Worship as Warfare

Conquering through the Sound of Surrender

Gerard Assey

Worship as Warfare:
Conquering through the Sound of Surrender

By
Gerard Assey

Published by:
Gerard Assey
19/18, Palli Arasan Street
Anna Nagar East
Chennai - 600 102

ISBN: 978-81-986974-5-5

Table of Contents

Disclaimer:

Any resemblance (names, characters, and scenarios used in this book, including testimonies and personal stories) to actual persons, living or dead, or actual events is purely coincidental. These examples are used solely for illustrative and teaching purposes.
The intent is to inspire and equip readers, not to depict real individuals or specific events. No harm or misrepresentation is intended.

Foreword

Why Worship Must Be Understood as Warfare

Dear Reader,

You didn't stumble upon this book by accident. I believe with all my heart that God is stirring the hearts of His people to rediscover worship—not merely as a spiritual expression but as a divine strategy for war.

In a time when the noise of the world grows louder and battles are fought in both visible and invisible realms, worship remains one of the most underutilized weapons in the believer's arsenal. We've often relegated it to the first 20 minutes of a church service or to a playlist we put on in the background during quiet time. But what if I told you worship was meant to break chains, silence enemies, overthrow strongholds, and shift atmospheres?

This book is not written from the comfort of a platform but from the trenches of life, where battles rage for our families, our churches, our cities, and our own souls. Worship is not the warm-up to war—it *is* war. It is not a moment; it is a posture. It is not entertainment; it is engagement.

I've watched lives radically transformed through worship—not just tears on cheeks, but healing in bones, clarity in minds, and demons driven out by nothing but the sound of surrendered praise. One young woman named Leena—whom you'll meet in a later chapter—sang through the darkest night of depression, and it was the very act of worship that opened the prison doors of her heart.

You are not just a spectator in a global battle between light and darkness. You are called to be a *worship warrior*. This book is your training ground. You will discover what worship truly is, what warfare really means, and why combining the two releases heaven's power on earth.

I pray that as you read, something awakens inside you—that you stop waiting for victory and start walking in it, not by striving, but by surrendering.
May your heart burn, your voice rise, and your life become a sound that makes hell tremble.

In His Presence and Power,

Introduction

What is Worship?

Worship is far more than a song. It is more than instruments, lyrics, or melodies. At its core, worship is a response to who God is and what He has done. It is the heart's posture before a holy God—a surrendering of self in reverence, awe, and love.

Biblically, worship is woven throughout the narrative of both the Old and New Testaments. In Genesis, Abel's offering was regarded as an act of worship—costly, pure, and pleasing to God (Genesis 4:4). Abraham demonstrated worship not with a song, but with obedience when he walked up Mount Moriah, prepared to sacrifice his son (Genesis 22:5). Worship is sacrifice. Worship is obedience. Worship is intimacy.

Jesus defined true worship when He said, "The hour is coming, and now is, when the true worshippers will worship the Father in spirit and truth" (John 4:23). It is spiritual and truthful, intimate and honest. Worship does not begin with sound—it begins with surrender. It is born in the heart, not the stage.

What is Warfare?

Warfare, in the context of Scripture, is not just physical—it is spiritual. The Apostle Paul makes this clear in Ephesians 6:12, where he writes, *"For we do not wrestle against flesh and blood, but against principalities, powers, rulers of darkness… spiritual hosts of wickedness in the heavenly places."*

Spiritual warfare is the unseen conflict that rages all around us. It is the battle for dominion—between the kingdom of God and the kingdom of darkness. Every temptation, every lie, every stronghold, every spiritual attack is part of this war.

Warfare is not always loud. Sometimes it looks like standing firm in faith, sometimes it's resisting fear, sometimes it's forgiving when it's hardest. It is not always external—it is often within.

Warfare is fought with weapons that are not carnal but mighty through God: truth, prayer, fasting, obedience—and yes, worship (2 Corinthians 10:4).

Why Worship as Warfare?

Because the two were never meant to be separated.

In the Bible, worship is often the method through which victory is released. In 2 Chronicles 20, when King Jehoshaphat's army was surrounded by enemies, God told them, *"You will not need to fight in this battle. Position yourselves, stand still and see the salvation of the Lord."* The Levites went out ahead of the army singing, *"Praise the Lord, for His mercy endures forever,"* and as they did, God set ambushes against their enemies (2 Chronicles 20:21–22).

Worship confuses the enemy. It shifts the atmosphere. It silences fear. Worship invites the King of Glory to step into our battles.

The truth is, when you worship in the face of worry, you are making war. When you choose praise over panic, obedience over offense, reverence over rebellion—you are fighting in the spirit.

Consider this:

Eliyan, a schoolteacher in a remote town, faced a mob that threatened her for being a Christian. That night, hiding in her home with her family, she lifted her trembling voice in worship. *"You are my hiding place,"* she sang, over and over. The mob eventually dispersed without harm. Weeks later, one of the men who had been there approached her in secret. *"When I heard you singing, it was as if fire surrounded your house. We could not come near."*

She didn't fight back with words or weapons—she fought back with worship.

When we sing, we often think we are simply expressing devotion. But in the spirit, we are drawing swords. We are releasing light. We are declaring allegiance. And that changes everything.

Misunderstandings and Misuse of Worship Today

Unfortunately, in our modern church culture, worship has often been misunderstood and misused.

For some, worship is performance. The lights, the band, the vocals—it's become about excellence, not presence. There's nothing wrong with excellence, but when it becomes entertainment rather than encounter, we have missed the mark.

For others, worship is emotionalism. The goal becomes tears rather than transformation. It's easy to associate the "feeling" of worship with its effectiveness, but worship isn't powerful because we cry—it's powerful because it aligns us with heaven.

Then there is the misconception that worship is passive. Many believers view worship as a "soft" activity, the emotional part of the service before the "real" stuff begins. But in Scripture, worship preceded walls falling (Joshua 6), kings bowing (Daniel 3), prisons breaking (Acts 16), and nations trembling.

Finally, there are those who reserve worship only for Sundays. True worshipers understand that what we do on Sunday is the overflow of what we live on Monday. Worship is a lifestyle—not a song list.

Consider Raghav, a 37-year-old investment banker who spent years finding his worth in success. Church was a ritual, and worship was something he endured until the sermon. But after a painful divorce and the collapse of his firm, Raghav began listening to worship alone in his apartment. At first, it was background noise. But one night, with no one watching, he lifted his hands and surrendered. That night, the war within him broke. God began to rebuild him from the inside out—not with sermons, but with song. Worship became his war cry.

This book is an invitation to return to the *heart* of worship, not as a genre or event, but as a *weapon*. You will learn how to wield it with reverence, how to live it with courage, and how to become a warrior whose battles are fought not with fists, but with fire from the throne of God.

SECTION I:
The Foundations of Worship as Warfare

Chapter 1:
Worship in the Beginning

The Origin of Worship: Eden and the Presence of God

In the beginning, before instruments, altars, and temples—before choirs, candles, or cathedrals—there was worship. It wasn't organized, choreographed, or rehearsed. It was the natural rhythm of a relationship between the Creator and His creation. Worship began in Eden.

Eden was not just a garden—it was a dwelling place. A sacred space where the presence of God met with the breath of man. The Bible tells us in Genesis 3:8 that God walked in the garden **"in the cool of the day."** This was not a symbolic visitation; it was literal, relational, intimate. Worship, in its purest form, was Adam and Eve living continually before the face of God—unashamed, uncovered, and unafraid.

There were no songs recorded in Eden, but there was *submission*. There was no liturgy, but there was *love*. There was no temple, but there was *truth*. Worship in Eden was not about a location—it was about communion. It was about presence.

But even in this divine setting, worship required something fundamental: alignment with God's will. The command not to eat from the tree of the knowledge of good and evil was not just about morality—it was about lordship. True worship has always involved the choice to honor God's rule above our own.

And this is where the war began.

The Fall and the Shift in Worship Dynamics

When Adam and Eve ate of the forbidden fruit, sin entered the world, and with it, a fracture in the foundation of worship. What had once been pure delight in God's presence was now contaminated by fear, shame, and hiding.

Genesis 3:8–10 says they *"hid themselves from the presence of the LORD God among the trees."* The very presence that once brought them joy now became a source of dread. This is the first picture of worship under warfare. The enemy's aim was not merely to cause a fall—it was to interrupt worship. To sever communion. To place self above surrender.

The serpent, Satan himself, knew the value of worship. Isaiah 14 describes his fall from heaven, when Lucifer, once a glorious worshiping angel, said in his heart, *"I will ascend…I will exalt…I will sit… I will be like the Most High."* (Isaiah 14:13–14). He craved the worship that belonged to God alone. That rebellion became the seed of all spiritual warfare. Worship has always been the battleground between pride and humility, flesh and spirit, rebellion and surrender.

After the fall, access to Eden was cut off. The presence of God, once freely accessible, was now protected by cherubim and a flaming sword (Genesis 3:24). From that moment, worship was no longer instinctual—it would have to be intentional. And with that shift, *worship became warfare.*

Cain and Abel: A Lesson in Worship Battles

The first recorded act of worship after the fall is found in Genesis 4. Two brothers—Cain and Abel—bring offerings to the Lord. One is accepted, and the other is rejected. On the surface, both men seem to be doing the right thing. They bring gifts to God. But God is not merely looking at the gift—He is looking at the heart.

"Abel also brought of the firstborn of his flock and of their fat. And the LORD respected Abel and his offering, but He did not respect Cain and his offering." (Genesis 4:4–5)

Why? Abel's offering was sacrificial, specific, and surrendered. Cain's offering, though from the fruit of the ground, lacked the heart posture of honor. It was worship on his terms, not God's.

This passage is not about fruit versus lambs. It's about the internal war of motives. Cain's heart was filled with entitlement, not adoration. And when his offering was rejected, jealousy and anger overtook him—so much so that he murdered his brother.

Worship became a battlefield again.

The Lord warned Cain: *"If you do well, will you not be accepted? And if you do not do well, sin lies at the door. And its desire is for you, but you should rule over it."* (Genesis 4:7). This is profound: God is showing us that the first fight in worship is the fight within ourselves—against pride, bitterness, jealousy, and control.

Cain lost that battle, not because his offering was inherently wrong, but because his heart refused correction. He desired the benefits of worship without the humility it requires.

Today, we often see this same war played out. A man named Ruben, a worship team leader in a bustling metropolitan church, had all the makings of a "successful worshipper"—a beautiful voice, a charismatic presence, and a growing following online. But when another team member, a quiet girl named Talia, was asked to lead a major event instead of him, Ruben spiraled into anger and offense. “I’ve been here longer,” he said bitterly to the pastor. “I’ve paid my dues.”

But what Ruben could not see was what Cain could not see: worship is not about recognition—it’s about reverence. His pride had turned a platform into a throne. And like Cain, he stood at the door of sin’s temptation.

In contrast, Talia, despite being nervous and unseen for years, offered up her leadership in fear and trembling. She spent nights in prayer, weeping before God. When she led, the atmosphere shifted—not because of her talent, but because her worship was a battle cry of surrender. Her sacrifice was accepted.

The Heavenly Picture: Revelation 4

To understand worship fully, we must look both to the beginning and to the end. Revelation 4 gives us a glimpse into the unceasing worship in heaven:

“Day and night they never stop saying: ‘Holy, holy, holy is the Lord God Almighty, who was, and is, and is to come.’” (Revelation 4:8)

Worship in heaven is *eternal*. It is the constant reality of heaven’s throne room. There is no war there—only victory. And yet, it is precisely this heavenly worship that informs our earthly warfare.

Why? Because when we worship here—especially in the middle of trials, pain, and pressure—we are joining heaven’s song against hell’s schemes. We are reminding principalities and powers that our allegiance is not to fear, flesh, or this fallen world—but to the Lamb upon the throne.

Heaven’s worship is our template. Earth’s battles are our context. Worship is the bridge.

Worship as the First Battleground

Worship was the first activity of creation and the first activity of rebellion. From Eden to Revelation, it has always been at the heart of the cosmic conflict between the kingdom of God and the kingdom of darkness.

Worship began in the presence. It was fractured by pride. It was tested through sacrifice. And it continues as the battleground of every believer's soul.

This is why worship is not optional for the Christian. It is not an accessory to our faith—it is the arsenal of our warfare.

In the chapters to come, we will walk through biblical examples, New Testament revelations, and real-life testimonies of worship as warfare. But let us never forget that it all began in a garden, with a God who walked with man and a war that started when that walk was broken.

And now, as redeemed children of God, we war in worship to walk with Him again.

Chapter 2:
Worship in Heaven: The First Battleground

Before the garden, before mankind, before the earth itself was formed—there was worship. Pure, radiant, and uninterrupted. Worship that resounded through the heavens, directed toward the One seated on the eternal throne. But even in that celestial realm, war broke out. And its origin? Worship gone wrong.

This chapter pulls back the curtain on the first rebellion, the one that split the heavens. It reveals how Lucifer, the anointed cherub, transformed from the most glorious worshipper to the originator of rebellion. And it teaches us that worship has always been more than song or sound—it is about authority, loyalty, and battle.

Lucifer's Rebellion – Pride in the Heart of a Worship Leader

The prophet Isaiah paints a vivid picture of Lucifer before his fall:

"How you are fallen from heaven,
O Lucifer, son of the morning!
How you are cut down to the ground,
You who weakened the nations!
For you have said in your heart:
'I will ascend into heaven,
I will exalt my throne above the stars of God…
I will be like the Most High.'"
— Isaiah 14:12–14 (NKJV)

Lucifer's fall was not over violence or immorality—but over worship. He was not content to lead worship; he wanted to receive it. His sin was subtle but devastating: pride. The very one designed to magnify God desired to magnify himself.

Ezekiel offers further insight into his original state:

"You were in Eden, the garden of God…
The workmanship of your timbrels and pipes
Was prepared for you on the day you were created.
You were the anointed cherub who covers;
I established you…
You were perfect in your ways
From the day you were created,
Till iniquity was found in you."
— Ezekiel 28:13–15

Lucifer was heaven's worship leader. His very being was fashioned for praise—music flowed from him. The "timbrels and pipes" were not instruments he played—they were instruments he was. He was a living symphony, created to glorify God.

But he shifted. He ceased to be a worshipper and became an idol—unto himself. What began as a celestial calling ended in cosmic corruption. And thus, the first war began in heaven—over worship.

What Heaven Teaches Us About the Nature of Worship and War

The moment Lucifer fell, heaven shifted from harmony to hostility. Revelation 12 gives us the clearest window into this heavenly war:

"And war broke out in heaven: Michael and his angels fought with the dragon; and the dragon and his angels fought, but they did not prevail, nor was a place found for them in heaven any longer." — Revelation 12:7–8

This is staggering. Heaven—the holiest of places—was not immune to conflict. The battleground was not over a territory, but over truth: Who is worthy of worship?

Lucifer's rebellion teaches us that worship is about allegiance. When he said, *"I will ascend… I will be like the Most High,"* he was declaring independence from God's authority. Worship, then, is not just about expression—it is about submission.

Heaven's response to rebellion was warfare. Michael, the archangel, and the armies of heaven rose up to drive out the traitor. This wasn't a passive negotiation. It was a decisive strike. Worship demanded war, and war secured the purity of worship again.

Lucifer, now Satan, was cast down—defeated, but still dangerous. His target ever since has been the worship of mankind. He cannot reclaim heaven, but he can pervert the praise of earth. Every temptation, every distraction, every idol he offers humanity is designed to redirect worship away from God.

Understanding this, we must realize: when we worship, we declare war on Satan's schemes. Every act of true worship is a threat to his kingdom. Every surrendered heart is a blow against his rebellion. Worship is not background music in the believer's life—it is battle strategy.

A Modern Echo: The Story of Amira

In a small North African village, a young woman named Amira was born into a household of devout ancestral tradition. Worship, in her home, meant appeasing spirits and performing rites inherited through generations. There was incense, chanting, and rituals—but never peace.

When Amira heard the gospel through a visiting teacher, something awakened in her. It wasn't just truth—it was freedom. She gave her heart to Christ quietly, whispering a prayer at night beneath the stars.

But the real war began after her conversion.

She stopped participating in the rituals. She no longer bowed before the ancestral shrines. Instead, she sang softly to Jesus under her breath while she cooked, cleaned, and cared for her siblings. Her worship, though private, was profound.

Her father, a fierce traditionalist, noticed the shift. One day, he confronted her: "You no longer respect the spirits! You bring disgrace!" He struck her across the face.

Amira didn't cry. She didn't shout. She closed her eyes and whispered, *"Jesus, I still love You."*

That night, her room filled with praise—no instruments, no music, just her voice. She sang of His faithfulness. And though her body bore bruises, her spirit was unshaken.

She didn't know it, but in heaven, angels moved. Her worship became warfare. Like Michael in Revelation, she fought with heaven's host—not against flesh and blood, but against spiritual forces in dark places. And victory was hers.

Years later, her father came to Christ. Not through argument, but through the unshakable worship of a daughter who refused to stop loving God.

Amira's story is not rare—it's a modern echo of an ancient battle. The war that began in heaven now plays out in every heart, every home, and every moment of worship.

Worship Is Always Contested

Lucifer fell because he wanted what belonged to God alone. Heaven went to war to protect what mattered most—God's glory. And even now, the same war rages on earth, not in politics or policies, but in hearts and altars.

When you choose to worship in truth and spirit, you take a stand. You declare whose side you're on. You invite heaven's armies to your defense. You confront the same rebellion Lucifer began.

This is why worship is warfare. It is not a genre. It is not a routine. It is the first and final battleground in the story of creation and redemption.

The question remains: will your worship echo heaven—or entertain hell?

Chapter 3:
Worship in the Wilderness

The wilderness is a place of testing, shaping, and revealing. For the Israelites, it was more than a dry and barren land—it was the classroom where they learned that worship was not just a ceremony, but the heartbeat of their identity and a key weapon in spiritual warfare.

God delivered Israel from slavery in Egypt not just to set them free from Pharaoh, but to bring them into relationship with Himself—marked by worship. *"Let My people go," He said through Moses, "so that they may worship Me"* (Exodus 8:1). This reveals a divine motive: liberation for the purpose of adoration.

But worship in the wilderness wasn't easy. It wasn't comfortable. And often, it was contested—by idolatry, fear, and spiritual forgetfulness. This chapter uncovers three powerful scenes: Mount Sinai, the wilderness Tabernacle, and the walls of Jericho. Through them, we learn that worship is warfare even when we feel lost, tired, or unworthy.

Israel's Journey: Worship as Identity, Warfare, and Witness

God did not bring Israel into the wilderness to abandon them, but to transform them. In Egypt, they were slaves. In Canaan, they would be warriors. But in the wilderness, they would learn to become worshippers.

At Sinai, God declared:

"Now if you obey me fully and keep my covenant, then out of all nations you will be my treasured

possession… You will be for me a kingdom of priests and a holy nation." — Exodus 19:5–6 (NIV)

This was identity-shaping language. God wasn't just giving them laws; He was forming a people whose primary calling was worship. Priests are worshippers. A holy nation lives to reflect God's glory.

In the wilderness, the Tabernacle became the center of Israel's life—not the war tent, not the political throne, but a mobile sanctuary. Worship was not peripheral. It was central. Wherever the cloud moved, the people moved. Their direction in life was determined by God's presence—not strategy, not survival.

The wilderness was never meant to be a permanent destination. But it was a proving ground—where worship would either deepen or die.

The Golden Calf vs. Tabernacle Worship

One of the most tragic contrasts in all of Scripture occurs in *Exodus 32*. Moses is on Mount Sinai, receiving the blueprint of the Tabernacle—God's detailed plan for worship. Meanwhile, at the base of the mountain, Aaron and the people are forging a golden calf, shouting and dancing in chaotic celebration.

"These are your gods, Israel, who brought you up out of Egypt." — Exodus 32:4

This was not worship—it was spiritual adultery. It was man-made, self-directed, and fueled by impatience and fear. They couldn't see Moses, so they made a god they could see. They wanted comfort more than communion. This act wasn't just idolatry—it was a rejection of warfare worship in exchange for counterfeit peace.

In contrast, Tabernacle worship required submission, holiness, reverence, and sacrifice. It wasn't wild. It was ordered. It was about encountering God on His terms. The Tabernacle was the place where blood met fire, where incense met intercession, and where obedience met presence.

This contrast reminds us: every heart is building something. Either a golden calf or a place for God's presence. There is no middle ground. True worship always costs something—your pride, your convenience, your agenda.

Warfare at Jericho: The Power of the Worship Shout

Fast forward forty years. The wilderness generation has died. Their children—raised on manna and miracles—are now poised to enter the Promised Land. And the first obstacle is Jericho, a walled fortress.

Joshua, their new leader, doesn't receive military tactics. He receives a worship strategy:

"Have seven priests carry trumpets of rams' horns in front of the ark. On the seventh day, march around the city seven times... When you hear them sound a long blast on the trumpets, have the whole army give a loud shout." — Joshua 6:4–5 (NIV)

This was not conventional warfare. It was prophetic warfare—led by worshippers, not warriors. The priests blew the shofar (trumpets), carrying the Ark of the Covenant. The Ark represented God's manifest presence—the heart of worship. And when the shout came, the walls fell.

No swords were drawn. No battering rams used. Worship won the war.

The worship shout at Jericho is not just noise—it's a declaration of victory before the battle is over. It's faith expressed in sound. It's heaven responding to human obedience.

A Wilderness Worshipper: The Story of Elijah Mendez

Elijah Mendez was a schoolteacher in a rural village in northern Peru. Known for his gentle nature and love for Scripture, Elijah was a quiet man—but not a timid one. His life changed when government pressure sought to shut down all "non-traditional religious gatherings." Elijah's small house church of twenty believers was deemed a "disturbance."

Threats came. His teaching license was revoked. Neighbors distanced themselves. For months, Elijah faced a wilderness—not of geography, but of isolation and fear.

But he didn't stop gathering. Instead of hiding, Elijah and his group gathered under a tree in the fields beyond the village. They brought no instruments—only voices. They sang psalms. They prayed. They recited Scripture in unison. They worshipped.

One evening, as the group worshipped under pouring rain, their voices rising like incense, something happened. A former official from the local government—known for opposing the church—watched them from a distance. Something pierced him. Days later, he sought Elijah out and asked, *"Why do you still sing? Why do you still smile?"*

Elijah replied softly, *"Because the wilderness doesn't change who I worship. It reveals why I must."*

The man wept. In time, he came to faith.

Worship in the wilderness is never wasted. Like Israel in the desert or Elijah in the rain, it shatters walls—spiritual and social—and testifies to a God who is present even in the dry places.

Learning to Worship When the Ground Is Dry

The wilderness is where idols are broken and intimacy is born. It is where the false gods we create are torn down and the true God becomes enough.

Worship is not reserved for sanctuaries and stages—it must rise from tents, deserts, and battlefields. In the wilderness, worship is identity, warfare, and witness. It tells heaven and hell alike that God is still enthroned, even when there is no manna, no water, and no crowd.

Whether you're marching around Jericho or weeping at the foot of Sinai, remember this: Worship is your weapon. Use it well.

Chapter 4: David – Warrior and Worshipper

David is one of the most complex and profound figures in Scripture. He was a shepherd, a poet, a warrior, and a king. But perhaps above all, David was a worshipper. His life reveals a truth that runs throughout all of Scripture: worship is not disconnected from warfare. It is the very center of it.

David's harp was not a performance instrument—it was a weapon in disguise. His psalms were not private musings; they were battle songs, forged in caves, on battlefields, and in the throne room of God. And his life teaches us that worship is not just a song—it's a stance.

David's Lifestyle: Harp and Sword

When we first meet David in *1 Samuel 16*, he is a young shepherd boy, overlooked even by his own family. Yet God sees in him something no one else does—a heart after His own. And when Saul is tormented by an evil spirit, it is David's harp, not Saul's army, that brings peace:

"And whenever the spirit from God came on Saul, David would take up his lyre and play. Then relief would come to Saul; he would feel better, and the evil spirit would leave him." — 1 Samuel 16:23 (NIV)

The harp was not just music—it was ministry. It was spiritual warfare. Darkness fled not from swords but from sacred sound. This is a picture of worship's power: it creates atmospheres that expel evil and enthrone God.

But David wasn't only a psalmist; he was a warrior. He killed lions and bears in secret, and giants in public. He led armies, conquered nations, and established Jerusalem as Israel's capital. Yet through it all, David never divorced worship from warfare. Whether in solitude or in strategy, his heart beat with the rhythm of heaven.

This is seen vividly in *2 Samuel 6*, when the Ark of the Covenant is brought into Jerusalem. David, wearing a linen ephod, dances before the Lord with all his might, humiliating himself before men but honoring God with reckless abandon.

"David danced before the Lord with all his might... leaping and dancing before the Lord."—2 Samuel 6:14,16 (NIV)

In this moment, David wasn't just rejoicing—he was reclaiming spiritual territory. Worship was making way for God's presence to reign in the city. It was public, passionate, and prophetic.

Psalms as Battle Songs

The Psalms are often seen as devotional literature, but they are far more than that. They are spiritual warfare manuals—expressions of lament, praise, declaration, and prophecy. David penned many of them in caves while fleeing Saul, in battle camps between wars, and in the temple courts during seasons of triumph.

Consider *Psalm 18*, written after the Lord delivered David from all his enemies:

"He trains my hands for battle; my arms can bend a bow of bronze... I pursued my enemies and overtook them; I did not turn back till they were destroyed." — Psalm 18:34, 37 (NIV)

This isn't poetry. It's warfare wrapped in melody. It reminds us that worship includes violent obedience against fear, despair, and spiritual enemies.

Or take *Psalm 144*:
"Praise be to the Lord my Rock, who trains my hands for war, my fingers for battle." — *Psalm 144:1 (NIV)*
The same hands that strummed strings in the sanctuary wielded swords in battle. The same fingers that played melodies also launched arrows. Worship wasn't separate from war. Worship *was* war.
David teaches us that to sing is not to retreat. It is to rise.

Spiritual Warfare Through Musical Expression
Worship is not emotion alone—it is a spiritual transaction. In David's life, musical expression was a conduit for divine power. The evil spirit that tormented Saul responded not to counsel, medication, or royal command—but to sound sanctified by the Spirit.
This is because music has always been a spiritual force. Lucifer, before his fall, was a being of sound and worship (Ezekiel 28:13). So when David played under the anointing, the atmosphere changed. Worship carries the authority to break spiritual oppression and assert heaven's will.
In today's world, where spiritual warfare often takes psychological and emotional forms, David's example is critical. Worship is not a filler before the sermon. It is an offensive strategy. When we lift our voices, we silence the enemy. When we play under the anointing, darkness trembles.

The Testimony of Aria Thompson
Aria Thompson was a single mother raising two sons in an urban neighborhood riddled with gang violence and spiritual apathy. She worked night shifts and could barely make ends meet. Church was her

refuge. But her home often felt like a battlefield—her younger son was battling depression; her older son was teetering toward gang influence.

Aria wasn't a pastor. She didn't lead worship on stage. But every night, after work, she would stand in the middle of her living room and sing. Sometimes in whispers. Sometimes through tears. Old hymns. Scriptures turned into melody. Her hands raised. Her voice steady. The presence of God would fill the room.

One night, as she sang Psalm 91 out loud, her older son came in from the streets. He paused, sat down, and said nothing. Night after night, he kept returning. One evening, as Aria played a recording of Psalm 27 set to music, her son broke. *"I don't know why, but when you sing that, I feel safe,"* he whispered.

That boy is now a worship leader in a church plant. Why? Because a mother chose worship as warfare.

Aria never preached a sermon. But like David, she played her harp in the dark, and giants fell.

The Heart That Fights and Sings

David's life reminds us that we do not have to choose between being worshippers and warriors. In God's kingdom, we are both. In fact, our most powerful victories often come when our sword is accompanied by a song.

Whether you're leading a church, raising children, or battling inner turmoil, worship is not optional. It is your weapon. David knew this. That's why, even on the battlefield, his harp was never far.

So raise your voice. Play your instrument. Write your psalms. Let your heart fight and sing. Because when worship rises, heaven invades, and the enemy retreats.

SECTION II:
Worship and Warfare in the New Covenant

Chapter 5: Jesus and Worship

To speak of worship in the New Covenant is to speak of Jesus. In Him, the mystery of worship is unveiled—not just as music or ceremony, but as *relationship*, *obedience*, *sacrifice*, and *warfare*. Jesus is the model worshipper: one who lived a life completely aligned with the heart of the Father. From the wilderness to Gethsemane to the cross, worship marked His every step.

Where Adam fell in the garden, Jesus stood firm in the wilderness. Where Israel faltered in their tests, Jesus triumphed. His worship was not about temple rituals or priestly robes—it was about authority, allegiance, intimacy, and unrelenting obedience. Through Jesus, we see worship not merely as an act of adoration, but as a *weapon against evil*, a *shield in suffering*, and a *pathway to resurrection power*.

Jesus' Temptation: Worship and Authority (Matthew 4:8–10)

One of the earliest glimpses we get of Jesus' spiritual warfare is during His temptation in the wilderness. After fasting for forty days, He is physically weak but spiritually alert. Satan approaches not with brute force, but with *subtle seduction*—offering shortcuts to glory, success, and kingship.

"Again, the devil took Him to a very high mountain and showed Him all the kingdoms of the world and their splendor. 'All this I will give you,' he said, 'if you will bow down and worship me.'" — Matthew 4:8–9 (NIV)

This was not merely a test of idolatry. It was a test of worship's allegiance. Satan didn't ask Jesus to build an altar. He asked Him to bow. That is what worship ultimately is—a *bowing of the will.* Satan was offering Jesus authority without the cross, power without suffering, a throne without submission.

But Jesus rebukes him:

"Away from me, Satan! For it is written: 'Worship the Lord your God, and serve Him only.'" — Matthew 4:10 (NIV)

This was not just resistance. It was *warfare through worship.* Jesus declares that true authority is rooted in worship of the One True God. The victory here wasn't just personal—it was cosmic. Jesus was reclaiming the authority Adam lost through misaligned worship in Eden.

Jesus at Gethsemane: Worship in the Face of Death (Matthew 26:36–46)

The garden of Gethsemane is where worship reaches its most agonizing form. Here, Jesus does not sing, lift His hands, or preach. He weeps. He sweats blood. He battles His own will in the shadow of the cross.

"My soul is overwhelmed with sorrow to the point of death… Father, if it is possible, may this cup be taken from Me. Yet not as I will, but as You will." — Matthew 26:38–39 (NIV)

Worship is surrender. It is not only the high notes of joy, but also the low groans of submission. In Gethsemane, we see Jesus choosing the Father's will over His own human longing for escape. This, too, is worship—perhaps its most intense form. He worships not by receiving, but by giving. Not by celebrating, but by yielding.

This is where many fall short. True worship does not end in the song service—it often begins in the *garden of decision*, where we say: “Not my will, but Yours be done.”

The Cross: Worship Through Obedience

The ultimate act of worship in human history happened not in a temple, but on a cross. It was not accompanied by music, but by cries of agony. It was not surrounded by praise, but by mockery. And yet, Jesus’ death was the most perfect expression of worship ever offered.

“And being found in appearance as a man, He humbled Himself by becoming obedient to death—even death on a cross!” — Philippians 2:8 (NIV)

Jesus showed that worship is not always accompanied by comfort or clarity. It is often obedience in pain, silence in injustice, and trust in God’s unseen plan.

On the cross, Jesus fulfilled the words He spoke to the Samaritan woman in John 4:

“A time is coming and has now come when the true worshippers will worship the Father in the Spirit and in truth…” — John 4:23 (NIV)

Spirit and truth met on the cross. And there, a new way of worship was born—not based on places, but on a Person. Not on rituals, but on relationship.

Worship in the Early Church (Acts 16:25–26)

The legacy of Jesus’ worship carried into the early church. Worship was no longer confined to the temple—it became a way of life, a means of warfare, and a declaration of Christ’s Lordship even in suffering.

Nowhere is this more vivid than in Acts 16, where Paul and Silas are imprisoned for preaching the Gospel. Their backs are bleeding, their feet are bound, and their future is uncertain. But instead of despair, they worship.

"About midnight Paul and Silas were praying and singing hymns to God, and the other prisoners were listening to them." — Acts 16:25 (NIV)

Then something supernatural happens:

"Suddenly there was such a violent earthquake that the foundations of the prison were shaken. At once all the prison doors flew open, and everyone's chains came loose."

— Acts 16:26 (NIV)

Worship here becomes earth-shaking warfare. Not only are Paul and Silas set free, but all the prisoners are loosed. This is what worship does—it shifts atmospheres, breaks chains, and opens doors.

Testimony of Marcus Leandro

Marcus Leandro was a former cartel member in a Latin American city. He was hardened by violence, betrayal, and deep spiritual oppression. But in a prison cell—serving a 40-year sentence—he found Christ. Or rather, Christ found him.

It began with a dream of a man on a cross whispering his name. When he awoke, a Christian inmate named Hector offered him a Bible. Days later, as Hector began to sing *"Amazing Grace"* in a broken voice, Marcus began to cry. He didn't understand the song, but he felt chains in his soul begin to tremble.

Eventually, Marcus joined in the worship. He learned to sing. To pray. To praise. Within a year, the prison warden noted a transformation so radical that he

gave Marcus permission to lead a nightly worship session in the cell block.
Violence decreased. Suicide rates dropped. Even guards would linger outside the walls during worship.
Worship, as Marcus later said in a testimony, "became my weapon, my healing, and my freedom."
Now released and leading a rehabilitation ministry, Marcus tells others: *"Don't wait for the chains to break to worship. Worship—and the chains will break."*

Jesus—the Worshipper Who Warred

Jesus did not merely teach worship; He lived it. In wilderness temptation, in garden agony, and on the cross, He showed us that worship is obedience under fire, surrender in sorrow, and authority over evil.
Worship in the New Covenant is no longer about location, but posture. No longer about rituals, but relationship. And no longer about survival, but victory.
So, whether you are in your wilderness, your Gethsemane, your prison cell, or your own cross-carrying season, remember: to worship is to war. To bow is to battle. And when you lift your voice in truth and Spirit, heaven will respond—and the earth will shake.

Chapter 6:
Paul and Silas – Worship in Chains

In a world where worship is often equated with comfort, aesthetics, and emotion, the story of Paul and Silas offers a jarring yet liberating perspective: worship can erupt in the darkest prison. Worship is not confined to grand cathedrals or musical perfection. Sometimes, its truest, rawest form echoes from the depths of suffering, layered with pain, uncertainty, and tears. This chapter explores the unforgettable midnight worship of Paul and Silas, and how that moment became a *heavenly earthquake* that shook both earth and eternity.

Worship in Suffering

The city of Philippi had been stirred into an uproar. Paul and Silas had delivered a slave girl from a spirit of divination, enraging her owners, who had profited from her bondage. Without trial or inquiry, the apostles were stripped, beaten, and thrown into the innermost part of the prison.

"After they had been severely flogged, they were thrown into prison, and the jailer was commanded to guard them carefully... he put them in the inner cell and fastened their feet in the stocks." — Acts 16:23–24 (NIV)

Everything about this situation screamed defeat—bruised backs, confined limbs, unjust treatment, and physical pain. And yet, verse 25 records something breathtaking:

"About midnight Paul and Silas were praying and singing hymns to God, and the other prisoners were listening to them." — Acts 16:25 (NIV)

Midnight. The symbolic hour when light is most absent and despair tempts the strongest hearts. But instead of cursing their pain or questioning their God, Paul and Silas *worshipped*. Their voices—perhaps cracking with exhaustion—rose in praise. Their songs, not of complaint, but of confidence.

This was not the worship of convenience; it was the worship of consecration. It was not about escape, but about intimacy with God amid pain.

In this moment, worship became warfare. Their suffering did not silence their faith—it sharpened it.

Earthquake Praise: The Supernatural Response

As Paul and Silas lifted their voices, something happened that no prison guard, no Roman magistrate, and not even they could have predicted:

"Suddenly there was such a violent earthquake that the foundations of the prison were shaken. At once all the prison doors flew open, and everyone's chains came loose." — Acts 16:26 (NIV)

The very earth responded. Not to rebellion. Not to riot. But to reverent worship. Praise carried such authority in that moment that it triggered a physical earthquake—God affirming that heaven was in agreement with what was happening.

But even more profound than the shaking ground was the breaking of chains. Not only Paul and Silas's chains, but *everyone's*. Worship is not a private experience; it has communal impact. When we choose to praise in our pain, others around us are often loosed as well.

There were no sermons preached that night, no elaborate arguments for the faith. There was only worship—and through it, an entire cell block experienced the power and presence of God.

How Worship Shifts Atmospheres

Worship changes more than hearts—it alters atmospheres. Before the earthquake came, something had already shifted in the spirit realm. The other prisoners were "listening" to Paul and Silas—not mocking, not jeering, but *drawn*. Something in the tone of their praise pierced the darkness.

There is a spiritual principle here: worship in suffering creates space for divine invasion. It is a declaration that even though circumstances may bind the body, they cannot chain the spirit.

The Story of Jonah Christopher

Jonah Christopher, a young man from Nairobi, was sentenced to life imprisonment at age 24 for a crime he did not commit. A quiet introvert, Jonah rarely spoke. For months he was isolated in prison, sinking into depression. One night, another inmate, Samuel, a former worship leader, was transferred into his cell. Samuel sang quietly to himself at night, often humming *"How Great Thou Art"* with tears in his eyes.

Jonah would lie in silence, listening.

One night, when the weight of despair became too much, Jonah broke down. Samuel invited him to sing with him. *"I don't know the words,"* Jonah said.

"Sing anything," Samuel replied. *"It's not the song—it's the cry."*

That night, Jonah sang his own simple words to God, unsure if they were heard. But something broke. His nightmares began to fade. The heaviness began to lift. Within two years, Jonah became a worship leader in prison. Eventually, new programs and testimonies of change led to a court re-evaluation. With the help of a pastor-advocate, Jonah was exonerated and released.

Today, Jonah travels across Africa sharing his story. He tells crowds, *"I worshipped God while still in chains—and it was there I discovered I was already free."*

The Jailer's Transformation

The story in Acts 16 doesn't end with open doors—it climaxes in a changed life.

"The jailer woke up, and when he saw the prison doors open, he drew his sword and was about to kill himself because he thought the prisoners had escaped." — Acts 16:27 (NIV)

But Paul stops him:

"Don't harm yourself! We are all here!" — Acts 16:28 (NIV)

This Roman jailer, hardened and likely indifferent to the prisoners' plight, was on the verge of suicide. But because of their worship—because they stayed when they could have run—he was saved. His first words:

"Sirs, what must I do to be saved?" — Acts 16:30 (NIV)

What a reversal. The jailer who bound them now begs for deliverance. The man who controlled their chains is now asking for the freedom they already possessed. And he receives it.

"They replied, 'Believe in the Lord Jesus, and you will be saved—you and your household.'" — Acts 16:31 (NIV)

He is baptized that night. He becomes a host of the Gospel, washing the wounds of the very men he imprisoned.

Chains Do Not Cancel Worship

The story of Paul and Silas teaches us this: chains may confine your body, but they cannot imprison your worship. Worship is a declaration of freedom before freedom comes. It is a song in the night that precedes the dawn. It is resistance against despair and partnership with the God who shakes prisons and sets captives free.

When we worship in chains—emotional, physical, relational, or spiritual—we enter into a divine paradox: what should break us becomes the very platform through which we break others free.

As believers in the New Covenant, we don't worship to get free—we worship because we are free. And in doing so, the chains fall—not just ours, but those of everyone listening.

Let your midnight song rise. Earth may tremble. Chains may fall. And lives may be saved.

Chapter 7: Worship as a Weapon Against Darkness

The battleground of the Christian life is not visible to the natural eye. Though we walk in the flesh, we do not wage war according to it. Beneath the veneer of human conflict, spiritual forces clash. Kingdoms contend for allegiance, souls, and destinies. In this invisible war, worship is not a retreat—it is a weapon. Worship, far from being just a musical expression or emotional escape, is a strategic act of spiritual resistance. It invites God's presence, establishes His rule, and disrupts demonic atmospheres. Throughout Scripture and even in our own day, we find that praise has the power to disarm darkness and usher in divine deliverance.

This chapter explores the power of worship against demonic resistance, its connection to the armor of God, and how praise becomes an active spiritual weapon.

Demonic Resistance to Worship

Lucifer was once heaven's worship leader. His downfall, as recorded in Isaiah 14 and Ezekiel 28, was rooted in pride. He sought to ascend the throne and receive the worship that belonged only to God. Ever since his expulsion from heaven, he has warred against true worship—because worship exalts the One he sought to dethrone.

In 2 Chronicles 20, we see a vivid picture of this warfare. Jehoshaphat, king of Judah, faced a vast and terrifying coalition of enemies—Moabites,

Ammonites, and Meunites. When news of the threat reached him, he did not summon generals or prepare war horses. Instead, he sought the Lord.

"Jehoshaphat stood in the assembly of Judah and Jerusalem in the temple of the LORD… and said: 'We do not know what to do, but our eyes are on You.'" — 2 Chronicles 20:5,12 (NIV)

The Spirit of the Lord came upon Jahaziel, a Levite, who gave a divine strategy:

"'Do not be afraid or discouraged… For the battle is not yours, but God's.'" — 2 Chronicles 20:15 (NIV)

What followed defied all logic:

"Jehoshaphat appointed men to sing to the LORD and to praise Him for the splendor of His holiness as they went out at the head of the army…" — 2 Chronicles 20:21 (NIV)

The choir led the army. As they sang, the Lord ambushed their enemies. Confusion broke out in the enemy camp. By the time Judah arrived, every enemy lay defeated—not by swords, but by songs.

Demonic forces resist worship because it dethrones them. Worship aligns hearts with heaven, disarms the lies of the enemy, and welcomes the King of glory to take His rightful place.

The Armor of God and Worship

In Ephesians 6:10–18, Paul writes his most famous passage on spiritual warfare. He reminds the church at Ephesus that their real struggle is not against "flesh and blood," but against *"the rulers… authorities… and powers of this dark world and spiritual forces of evil in the heavenly realms."*

Then comes the command: put on the full armor of God. Each piece of armor is a truth-bound, gospel-centered declaration:

- ✓ *The belt of truth*
- ✓ *The breastplate of righteousness*
- ✓ *The shoes of the gospel of peace*
- ✓ *The shield of faith*
- ✓ *The helmet of salvation*
- ✓ *The sword of the Spirit (the Word of God)*

And yet, Paul closes the passage with a command often overlooked:

"And pray in the Spirit on all occasions with all kinds of prayers and requests… be alert and always keep on praying…" — Ephesians 6:18 (NIV)

Worship, as an act of spiritual alignment, undergirds all these pieces. It reminds us of truth. It stirs our faith. It proclaims salvation. It unleashes the Word. Worship doesn't replace the armor—it activates it.

The Story of Nia Thomas

Nia Thomas, a schoolteacher in New Orleans, found herself under intense spiritual oppression following the sudden death of her husband. Though a believer, she began experiencing nightly torment—sleep paralysis, overwhelming fear, and vivid nightmares. She tried prayer and Scripture reading but felt no breakthrough.

One evening, broken and exhausted, she turned on a worship album by a missionary friend and simply whispered, *"Jesus, I don't know how to fight. But I know how to love You."* She began singing softly. At first, it was through tears. Then, something shifted.

The air in the room changed. A peace entered that she hadn't felt in months. Night after night, she continued—singing, declaring Scriptures, playing worship softly as she slept.

Three weeks later, all torment stopped. No more sleep paralysis. No more fear. Nia now leads a women's group teaching spiritual warfare through worship. She tells them, *"When I couldn't fight in the flesh, I won with my voice. My worship was my armor."*

Praise as a Spiritual Weapon

Psalm 149 is a psalm of praise and warfare. It begins with the joy of singing a new song and ends with stunning authority:

"May the praise of God be in their mouths and a double-edged sword in their hands, to inflict vengeance on the nations and punishment on the peoples, to bind their kings with fetters, their nobles with shackles of iron, to carry out the sentence written against them—this is the glory of all His faithful people." — Psalm 149:6–9 (NIV)

Worship binds the enemies of God—not by physical chains, but by spiritual fetters. Praise is not passive; it is prophetic. It declares the victory of God before the battle is won. It confronts darkness not with fear, but with faith.

The Testimony of Eladio Hernandez

Eladio, a former gang leader from Guadalajara, was radically saved in prison after hearing the gospel from a chaplain. Upon his release, he began ministering to young men involved in drug trafficking. He faced death threats, was chased by rival factions, and narrowly escaped three ambushes.

What kept him steady was worship.

Before every outreach, Eladio would gather his small team and lead them in songs—songs in Spanish declaring God's sovereignty, His power, His love. Sometimes, they would sing in front of abandoned buildings, in gang-controlled zones, with nothing but a guitar and trembling voices.

He tells the story of one night when they entered a cartel-infested neighborhood. As they began to worship, two men with machetes approached, but suddenly stopped—frozen. One of them later confessed that when they began singing, he “saw flames” surrounding them and couldn’t move.

Eladio says, “*We didn’t bring guns. We brought glory. And glory always wins.*”

Singing in the Face of Darkness

The enemy fears worship not because of sound but because of submission. True worship exalts God and dethrones evil. It reminds Satan that he has lost. It reclaims territory for the kingdom. It silences fear, breaks chains, and opens the heavens.

Worship is not a warm-up. It is warfare.

So when darkness surrounds you, don’t shrink back. Sing. Declare. Praise. Proclaim the greatness of God with the authority given to you in Christ. Let worship be the sound that shakes your soul free.

Like Jehoshaphat, Paul and Silas, and countless unnamed saints across the ages, raise your voice. Worship with your mouth. War with your praise.

Because sometimes, the most powerful thing you can do is sing in the dark.

SECTION III:
Becoming a Worship Warrior

Chapter 8: Characteristics of a Worship Warrior

Romans 12:1–2, John 4:23–24

To become a true worshipper who wars in the spirit, one must not simply sing songs or lift hands in church services. A *Worship Warrior* is not defined by performance but by posture—an inward yielding that manifests outwardly through powerful, Spirit-led worship. This kind of worship dismantles demonic strongholds, shifts spiritual atmospheres, and invokes divine intervention. Romans 12:1–2 urges us to *present our bodies as a living sacrifice*, which is our reasonable act of worship. In John 4:23–24, Jesus proclaims that the Father seeks those who worship in *spirit and truth*. The heart of a worship warrior is formed by brokenness, boldness, intimacy, sensitivity, and obedience—each one a trait forged in God's presence, not on a stage.

Brokenness and Boldness: The Paradox of Power

A worship warrior lives in the paradox of brokenness and boldness. Brokenness is not weakness; it is surrender. Boldness is not arrogance; it is confidence in God's authority.

Biblical Example: Hannah's Worship (1 Samuel 1–2) Hannah's tears at the temple were not a performance—they were pure, heart-wrenching worship. Her barrenness broke her, but in that brokenness, she came before God with such boldness that Eli thought she was drunk. Her bold request was answered with Samuel, and her prayer in 1 Samuel 2 became a prophetic song of victory. Her brokenness was the soil where boldness grew, and her worship turned her pain into prophecy.

Real-life Example: Grace Elijah

Grace was a shy, introverted nurse in a rural village. After the death of her son in a sudden accident, she withdrew completely. Her grief isolated her, but one night in her small prayer room, she broke down before God—not with words, but with sobbing worship. Over time, her intimacy with the Lord was reborn. Grace began to sing again, alone at first, then at home groups, then at the hospital chapel. As she sang, patients wept, and doctors paused. It was not her voice but the authority in her worship. Grace, once broken, now stood boldly as a vessel of healing and deliverance through worship.

Intimacy with God: The Core of the Worship Warrior

Worship is not for an audience of thousands, but for an Audience of One. A worship warrior's strength comes from abiding in the secret place with God, not in the noise of public adoration.

Biblical Example: Moses and the Tent of Meeting (Exodus 33:7–11) Moses would enter the Tent of Meeting, and *the Lord would speak to him face to face, as a man speaks with his friend*. Joshua stayed behind even after Moses left. It was in these intimate moments that Moses' face would shine with God's glory. Worship warriors are forged in solitude, where intimacy becomes identity.

Real-life Example: Joel Mathias

Joel was a worship leader at a growing city church, but burnout and bitterness had crept into his soul. Songs felt like scripts, and Sundays became rehearsals. One weekend, he took a silent retreat in the mountains. With no instruments or agendas, Joel simply sat before God. He repented, wept, and listened. In that intimate place, God restored his heart. Joel's songs changed. They became whispers of heaven rather than echoes of trends. His private intimacy restored his public anointing.

Sensitivity to the Holy Spirit: Responding to Divine Movement

A worship warrior does not lead—he follows. The Holy Spirit is the conductor, and the worshipper is merely an obedient instrument. Sensitivity to the Spirit distinguishes a performer from a warrior.

Biblical Example: Philip and the Ethiopian Eunuch (Acts 8:26–40)

Though not a worship set in the musical sense, this moment teaches us the importance of Spirit-led responsiveness. Philip was worshipping through obedience. The Spirit told him to approach the chariot, and he obeyed. His sensitivity led to the salvation and baptism of the Ethiopian. Worship that is led by the Spirit always results in transformation.

Real-life Example: Leya Kurien

Leya was leading a worship set at a women's conference when she felt the Spirit prompt her to pause mid-song. She stood silent, unsure at first, but obeyed. A minute passed, then two. In the stillness, a woman in the audience screamed and fell to her knees. She had been contemplating suicide but, in that silence, heard the Lord say, "I see you." Leya's sensitivity to the Holy Spirit wasn't flashy, but it was fierce. That moment became a breakthrough for many. The Spirit is not always loud, but He is always leading.

Obedience Over Performance: The Sacrifice God Desires

Worship without obedience is hollow. True worship warriors value God's instructions more than their own inclinations. Saul lost his throne because he chose performance over obedience (1 Samuel 15:22). The Father is not impressed by talent, but He is moved by trust.

Biblical Example: Abraham and Isaac (Genesis 22)

Abraham's willingness to sacrifice Isaac was worship at its most raw and costly. The journey to Moriah was not just an act of faith—it was a worship march. His obedience became a declaration that God was worthy even above his promise. Worship warriors lay everything down, trusting God with the outcome.

Real-life Example: Rachel D'Costa

Rachel was offered a national recording contract after her song went viral. But during prayer, she felt the Lord say, "Not yet." Against advice and ambition, she said no. For two years, she served as a volunteer worship leader in a children's hospice. One day, a dying child asked her to sing the same viral song. In that room, worship filled the atmosphere, and the child passed peacefully. Rachel understood: the value of her worship wasn't in platforms, but in obedience. Obedience will always take you places that applause never can.

A Living Sacrifice: Becoming the Weapon

Romans 12:1–2 calls us to present our bodies as living sacrifices—holy and pleasing to God. This is true worship. Worship warriors live consecrated lives. They do not conform to the patterns of this world but are transformed by the renewing of their minds. The

battlefield is not always outside; often, it is within. It is in the daily choices, the hidden motives, the quiet obedience.
In John 4, Jesus reveals that true worship is not about location or tradition—it's about spirit and truth. Worship warriors are those who have aligned their entire lives—thoughts, words, actions—with God's truth, empowered by the Spirit. Their worship is warfare because it testifies to another kingdom, another King, and another reality.

The Worship Warrior's Path

To become a worship warrior is not to master music or memorize scripture. It is to offer oneself fully to God, broken but bold, intimate yet obedient, sensitive and surrendered. A worship warrior doesn't just sing battlesongs—they live them. Their life is the altar, and their praise is the fire that invites the God of heaven to wage war on their behalf.
This is not a calling for a few—it is the destiny of all God's people. When we worship, we war. When we bow low, heaven rises high. When we cry holy, hell trembles.
Let every reader rise—not just as a singer, but as a warrior.
Let every life become a weapon of worship.

Chapter 9: Enemies of Worship

Amos 5:21–24, Matthew 15:8–9

Worship is a sacred exchange—an intimate moment where the finite touches the Infinite, where earth surrenders to heaven, and where a heart aligns with the will of God. But this sacred exchange is constantly under assault. Not from outside the church, but from within. The enemies of worship are subtle and sly, often clothed in what appears spiritual but lacks the substance of spirit and truth. True worship calls for authenticity, brokenness, and surrender. Anything that attempts to counterfeit or contaminate this exchange becomes an enemy of worship.

God's words in Amos 5:21–24 are thunderous and sobering: *"I hate, I despise your feast days… Take away from Me the noise of your songs… But let justice run down like water, and righteousness like a mighty stream."* These are not the words of a distant, angry deity—but of a holy God who will not be mocked by hollow performance. Similarly, in Matthew 15:8–9, Jesus repeats Isaiah's prophecy: *"These people honor Me with their lips, but their hearts are far from Me. They worship Me in vain."*

Let us then confront the hidden assassins of worship. Not with judgment, but with discernment and repentance. For to worship rightly, we must first clear the altar of everything false.

The Enemy of Distraction

Worship demands focus. It is the discipline of giving undivided attention to the One who alone is worthy.

But distraction pulls our gaze away—not always to sin, but to the trivial. The heart of a distracted worshipper is cluttered, making it hard to recognize God even when He is present.

Biblical Example: Martha and Mary (Luke 10:38–42)

Jesus entered their home, and Martha busied herself with the preparation. She was doing something good, yet missed the better thing. Mary, on the other hand, sat at His feet, giving Him her full attention. Distraction is not always about sin; often, it's about choosing good over God. In worship, we are not called to perform for Jesus—we are called to sit at His feet.

Real-life Example: Kevin D'Mello

Kevin was a media technician at a large city church. He would arrive early, adjust sound levels, coordinate slides, and ensure every frame was perfect. But over time, his work became his worship. One Sunday, during a worship session, the lead projector failed. Kevin rushed to fix it but found himself frozen, watching the congregation with arms lifted high. He felt a whisper in his soul: *"When did you stop worshipping Me and start working for Me?"* That moment changed everything. Kevin restructured his tasks, ensuring that before he served, he worshipped. Distraction, even in ministry, can rob us of the main thing—His presence.

The Enemy of Pride

Pride is the most deceptive enemy of worship because it can wear the robe of spiritual success. It places self on the throne instead of God. Pride craves recognition, applause, and spiritual status.

True worship, however, demands humility—it is the act of bowing low so that God may be lifted high.

Biblical Example: King Uzziah (2 Chronicles 26)

Uzziah started well, seeking God, and prospered. But when he became strong, his heart was lifted in pride. He entered the temple to burn incense, a task only for the priests. Though warned, he refused to repent, and God struck him with leprosy. Uzziah's pride corrupted his worship, and the presence he once honored became a place of judgment.

Real-life Example: Anita George

Anita was a charismatic worship leader whose voice captivated crowds. Invitations flooded in from conferences and crusades. Over time, she began to measure her success by applause, social media reach, and compliments. One night, while rehearsing before a major event, she lost her voice. No illness, no warning—just silence. Weeks passed without recovery. In the quiet, God showed her the pride that had replaced purity. She wept, repented, and laid down her microphone. Six months later, her voice returned. But this time, her song carried brokenness. It wasn't as strong, but it was anointed. Pride had stolen her worship. Repentance restored it.

The Enemy of Tradition

Tradition, when unexamined, can become a chain that binds rather than a bridge that connects. While some traditions preserve reverence, others can fossilize faith. When tradition becomes more important than truth, we worship methods over the Master.

Biblical Example: The Pharisees (Matthew 15:8–9)

Jesus confronted the religious leaders for elevating their traditions above God's commands. Their lips moved in reverence, but their hearts were distant. Their ceremonies were exact, but their spirits were empty. True worship cannot flow from formulas—it flows from relationship.

Real-life Example: Dr. Benedict Samuel

Benedict was raised in a historic cathedral. Every Sunday, worship followed a rigid sequence—processions, recitations, liturgy. He became a priest, faithfully preserving the structure. But something inside him longed for more. On a sabbatical in Africa, he visited a rural church where worship was raw, unrefined, yet radiant. People danced barefoot, cried aloud, and prayed with fire. No robes, no rituals—just presence. He realized he had worshipped tradition more than Truth. Returning home, he began to lead with both reverence and release, combining the beauty of ancient forms with the freedom of the Spirit.

The Enemy of Self

Perhaps the greatest rival to worship is self—self-importance, self-interest, self-preservation. When worship becomes about what we *get* instead of what we *give*, it ceases to be worship at all. Worship is not about us—it's about Him.

Biblical Example: Saul's Disobedience (1 Samuel 15:10–23)

Saul was instructed to destroy everything, but he kept the best of the spoils. When confronted, he said it was "to sacrifice to the Lord." God saw through the pretense. "To obey is better than sacrifice." Saul's worship was about self-preservation—he feared the people more than he honored God. And in that moment, the kingdom was torn from him.

Real-life Example: Nilesh Abraham

Nilesh loved worship because it made him *feel* something. He would chase bands, new songs, and emotional highs. But when his prayers went unanswered, he grew cold. One evening, alone in his room, he asked, "God, why don't I feel You anymore?" A still voice replied, *"Because you were worshipping your emotions, not Me."* That realization hit hard. Nilesh began to worship, not for a feeling, but in faith. Over time, he discovered deeper joy—one not tied to mood, but to the unchanging character of God.

False Worship: Entertainment vs. Encounter
The modern worship movement has brought many blessings, but also many pitfalls. A dark seduction creeps in when lights, sound, and style become the focus rather than Spirit-led surrender. Worship becomes a concert instead of a consecration. It entertains the crowd rather than engages the King.
Biblical Echo: Amos 5:23
"Take away from Me the noise of your songs, for I will not listen to the melody of your harps." God does not delight in noise, no matter how beautiful, if it lacks righteousness.
Real-life Example: Melody Rosario
Melody directed the worship experience at a megachurch. Every Sunday was a production—LED screens, timed lights, rehearsed transitions. It drew crowds, but over time, the weight of it felt hollow. One morning, a technical glitch forced the team to abandon all visual effects. Left with just a guitar and a prayer, they worshipped anyway. What followed was raw, unscripted, and sacred. People wept, repented, danced, and lingered long after service.

That day, they encountered God—not through effects, but through authenticity.

Idolatry in Modern Worship

Idolatry is not always a golden calf. Sometimes, it's a golden microphone. When leaders are worshipped more than the Lord, when songs replace scripture, when performance outshines presence, idolatry has taken root. God shares His glory with no one.

Biblical Example: Aaron and the Golden Calf (Exodus 32)

While Moses was on the mountain in communion with God, the people grew restless. They asked for a god they could see. Aaron gave in and fashioned a golden calf. They danced around it, calling it "the god who brought us out of Egypt." They attributed God's glory to a manmade thing. How often do we, unknowingly, do the same in modern worship?

Real-life Example: Judah Matthew

Judah was a gifted worship artist whose albums topped Christian charts. With fame came adoration. His fans praised him more than the God he sang about. Slowly, Judah began to feed off the fame. He rarely prayed, didn't read scripture, and only worshipped during studio recordings. One night, after a performance, he knelt backstage and heard the Lord say, *"You've become what they worship."* That moment broke him. He took a sabbatical, stepped away from the spotlight, and found Jesus again in silence. Today, he leads small house worship nights with no stage—just a circle, a candle, and a heart that truly burns.

Clearing the Altar

Worship is not an act; it is a life. But like any altar, it must be cleared of impurities. Distraction, pride, tradition, and self must be cast off. Entertainment must give way to encounter. Idols must be shattered. For God is still seeking worshippers—true ones—who will worship in spirit and in truth.

Let each reader examine their own altar. Let every worshipper fall on their face before God and ask: *"Is this for You, or is it for me?"* For in that question lies the difference between empty ritual and divine encounter.

Let us not offer noise when He asks for justice.

Let us not present performance when He desires surrender.

Let us not give Him half our hearts when He deserves it all.

Let us worship—not as spectators, but as sacrifices.

Not as fans of worship, but as true friends of God.

Chapter 10:
Real-Life Testimonies

Worship as a Weapon of Victory

Throughout the ages, worship has been far more than just a melodious offering. It has been a battleground of faith, a weapon in spiritual warfare, and a doorway to divine encounter. The pages of Scripture are filled with stories where worship turned the tide—from Jehoshaphat's victory through praise (2 Chronicles 20) to Paul and Silas singing in prison and watching the doors swing open (Acts 16:25–26). But these weren't just ancient tales. Even today, in modern cities and obscure villages, worship continues to heal, break chains, silence suicidal thoughts, and reconcile broken families. This chapter brings to light a few powerful testimonies of ordinary believers who encountered an extraordinary God through the gift of worship.

1. Miriam Joseph – The Night Music Saved Her Life

Miriam Joseph was a 27-year-old banker in Mumbai, India. Behind her carefully curated Instagram life and sharply dressed corporate appearance, she carried scars invisible to the world. Years of sexual abuse in her early teens, coupled with the sudden death of her younger brother in a road accident, had torn gaping holes in her soul. Therapy helped for a season, but darkness always found a way to creep back.

On a humid Friday evening, Miriam stood on the edge of her high-rise apartment's balcony, ready to end her life. As she stared down at the city's moving lights, a soft melody began to play inside her room.

Her roommate had left a worship playlist on shuffle. The lyrics that suddenly pierced the silence were from a simple, old hymn: "Turn your eyes upon Jesus, look full in His wonderful face…"

For reasons she couldn't explain, Miriam froze. Her tears stopped. Her heart, which had been racing uncontrollably, began to calm. She stepped back inside and collapsed on the floor, weeping—not from despair this time, but from the strange sense of peace that washed over her.

That night, she didn't die. That night, she lived. In the weeks that followed, Miriam began attending a small house church where worship was raw, vulnerable, and authentic. It wasn't entertainment—it was encounter. Through nights of tears and lifted hands, she found healing in the presence of the One who had never left her side. Like David in Psalm 40:2–3, she declared later, *"He lifted me out of the slimy pit... He put a new song in my mouth, a hymn of praise to our God."*

2. Kwame and Elsie Nkrumah – When Worship Healed a Home

Kwame Nkrumah was a successful engineer in Accra, Ghana. His wife, Elsie, a primary school teacher, was known for her cheerful nature and godly demeanor. But their marriage, despite its joyful public image, was on the brink of collapse. Kwame had secretly battled pornography addiction for over a decade—a secret that eventually came to light and shattered Elsie's trust.

After several months of cold silence and counseling that seemed to go nowhere, they decided to take a break. Elsie moved to her sister's house with their two daughters. One Sunday, alone in his living room,

Kwame began to sing—not out of ritual, but out of desperation. It was a simple tune, a Ghanaian worship chorus that his grandmother used to sing over him as a child: *"Nyame ye o, Nyame ye (God is good, God is good)."*

As he worshipped, he found himself on the floor, sobbing. The song became his cry. Over the next few days, he made worship a daily practice—not to earn forgiveness, but to allow God to break and rebuild him. The addiction lost its grip in the furnace of worship. The Spirit of God brought repentance, not just remorse. He wrote a letter to Elsie, not asking her to return, but to tell her what the Lord had done in him.

Elsie, too, had been worshipping during her quiet evenings. Songs became her balm and her sword. One evening while singing, *"He makes all things new,"* she felt the Holy Spirit prompt her to begin again.

Their family now leads worship at their local church, and their testimony has helped dozens of other couples find healing. Just as in Acts 16, where an earthquake broke prison chains, worship shook the foundations of their broken marriage and built something stronger in its place.

3. Isaiah Lin – The Addict Who Found Freedom Through the Psalms

Isaiah Lin grew up in the outskirts of Taipei, Taiwan. He was the son of devout Christians but had strayed early in life. At 19, he fell into drug use that spiraled into years of heroin dependency. Arrested twice, estranged from his family, and homeless, Isaiah found himself in a Christian rehabilitation center run by missionaries.

On his second day there, a volunteer handed him a Bible and an old guitar. He scoffed at both. But that night, unable to sleep, he opened the Bible randomly and landed on Psalm 18:6: *"In my distress I called to the Lord... He heard my voice."*

He didn't understand everything, but those words felt alive. Slowly, he began to strum simple chords on the guitar. He found himself singing the Psalms. They became his prayers. They became his medicine. His favorite became Psalm 51—David's cry for mercy. As he sang it daily, the withdrawal symptoms grew weaker, and a new strength rose inside him.

Months passed. Isaiah stayed clean. He began writing his own worship songs, deeply rooted in Scripture. Eventually, he became part of the rehab center's leadership. His story, much like the demoniac of the Gadarenes who was set free and later sent to tell his people (Mark 5:19), is now shared in local churches as a living testament to the power of worship and the living Word.

4. Sofía Delgado – The Missionary Who Danced in the Fire

Sofía Delgado was a 35-year-old missionary from Bogotá, Colombia, serving in remote parts of Ethiopia. When political tensions rose in the region, foreigners were warned to leave. But Sofía stayed behind to serve the women and children she had grown to love.

One night, rebels raided the village. Sofía and a few others were locked in a hut for three days without food. Fear was thick. But on the second night, something unusual happened. Sofía began to sing quietly. At first it was almost inaudible, but then louder: *"You are my hiding place, You always fill my heart with songs of deliverance…"*

The others joined in. Soon the small hut was filled with voices worshipping in Spanish, Amharic, and English. That night, guards reported hearing "unexplainable singing" and seeing "light" coming from the hut. By morning, the rebels had left the village without harming a soul.

To this day, locals refer to that night as "The Night the Angels Sang." Sofía testifies that worship was not just her survival—it was her shield. Like Paul and Silas, her worship didn't just free her; it influenced everyone around her.

5. Jared Monroe – The Intercessor with the Broken Voice

Jared Monroe was never meant to be a worship leader. He was a behind-the-scenes prayer warrior, soft-spoken and plain in appearance. Born with a vocal cord issue, Jared stuttered terribly and couldn't hold a tune. But he loved the presence of God. And he worshipped with everything he had.

One evening at a prayer vigil, the worship team was late. Jared was asked to start. Reluctantly, he stepped up and began to sing a chorus he had written during his prayer time. To everyone's shock, as he sang, his stutter vanished. His voice, though not perfect, carried weight and authority.

That night sparked a change in Jared. He began leading worship in small groups, not because of his voice but because of his intimacy with God. People often wept during his songs—not from musical excellence, but from the presence that came with it.

His life echoes the words of 1 Samuel 16:7: *"Man looks at the outward appearance, but the Lord looks at the heart."* Jared is now a mentor to other worshippers and a reminder that worship isn't about performance—it's about surrender.

The Testimony of Jesus Is the Spirit of Prophecy

As Revelation 19:10 says, *"The testimony of Jesus is the spirit of prophecy."* These stories—of suicide halted, marriages restored, addictions broken, villages saved, and voices healed—are not just heartwarming; they are prophetic. They speak of what God still desires to do in and through our worship today.

Worship is not a filler before the sermon. It is war. It is healing. It is communion. These testimonies remind us that when we sing, we are not merely echoing lyrics—we are declaring truth, pushing back darkness, and opening our hearts to a God who is still in the business of miracles.

SECTION IV:
A Practical Guide to Cultivating Worship as Warfare

Chapter 11:
The Daily Altar – Personal Worship Habits

Creating Sacred Spaces in the Ordinary

In the ancient world, altars were sacred places of encounter. Abraham built an altar each time God revealed Himself. Isaac returned to the altars his father built. Jacob wrestled with God and named the place "Bethel"—House of God. These altars weren't ornamental; they were declarations of trust, surrender, and intimacy.

In the New Covenant, we no longer build altars with stones—we become the altar (Romans 12:1). Our hearts are the new sacred space where worship rises daily, not just on Sundays. Worship as warfare must not be occasional. It must be a lifestyle—consistent, intentional, and deeply personal.

This chapter is about building your daily altar—not in public meetings, but in the privacy of your soul where God sees, meets, and transforms you.

How to Build a Lifestyle of Worship

A lifestyle of worship is not simply about music. It's about posture—of the heart, mind, and soul. It is aligning every part of your life with the supremacy of Christ. Just as Daniel opened his window and prayed three times a day, worshipping in defiance of Babylon's pressure (Daniel 6:10), a lifestyle of worship is deliberate. It becomes our resistance against spiritual passivity.

Caleb Munroe – Worship in the Midst of Chaos

Caleb Munroe was a firefighter in the Bronx, New York. He had seen tragedies up close: burnt homes, children in pain, lives shattered in seconds. It left scars. PTSD symptoms crept in—nightmares, emotional distance, guilt. Caleb, though raised in church, felt far from God.

One evening, while resting after a difficult rescue, he opened his phone and played a worship instrumental track. He didn't sing. He didn't even pray. He just let the music fill the silence. It became a ritual. Before every shift, he played one song. Slowly, the chaos around him stopped controlling the storm within.

Worship didn't change his job—it changed his *reality*.

Today, Caleb mentors other first responders, teaching them how to build "quiet altars" even in the noisiest environments. He often quotes Psalm 91:1:

"He who dwells in the secret place of the Most High shall abide under the shadow of the Almighty."

Worship, done daily, becomes a dwelling—not a drive-thru encounter.

Quiet Time Strategies

Jesus, though pressed by crowds and constantly pursued, often withdrew to "lonely places" to be with the Father (Luke 5:16). His ministry flowed from His solitude. So should ours.

- ✓ Set a Time and Keep It Sacred
  Consistency matters more than duration. Whether it's fifteen minutes at dawn or half an hour at night, protect it. Set an appointment with God as you would with your dearest friend.
- ✓ Create Atmosphere

It may be a chair by the window, a small corner with a candle, or a playlist that sets the tone. Let that space become your sacred ground. Over time, your spirit will begin to anticipate and yearn for those moments.

Arpita Roy – A Song at 5:45 AM

Arpita Roy was a single mother in Kolkata, juggling two jobs and raising her young son. Her schedule was a whirlwind. She felt guilty for not spending enough time in prayer. One morning, she simply woke up fifteen minutes earlier, put on a soft Bengali worship chorus, and sat quietly with her Bible open.

She didn't speak much. She just listened. Over time, 5:45 AM became her sacred hour. God began to meet her in the simplicity of her surrender. Joy returned. Strength was renewed. Her son, just five, started sitting beside her, humming along. One morning he whispered, "Mom, I feel happy when we sing."

That was her reward. Like Mary sitting at Jesus' feet (Luke 10:39), she chose the "better part," and it changed the atmosphere of her home.

Making Room for God's Presence

The presence of God is not limited to temples or cathedrals. When we make room, He comes. Elisha, the prophet, often stayed with a Shunammite woman who prepared a small room for him—just a bed, a table, a chair, and a lamp (2 Kings 4:10). It became a chamber of miracles.

The same principle applies spiritually. When you prepare space in your schedule, heart, and mind, you are telling God: *"You are welcome here."*

Julian Vega – A Room That Changed Everything

Julian Vega was a high school music teacher in Manila. He struggled with anxiety, especially before major school performances. One night, overwhelmed and unable to sleep, he opened his closet, sat down cross-legged, and whispered, "Lord, I don't know what I'm doing, but I need You."

That closet became his prayer room. Every morning before work, he sat there for ten minutes, sometimes weeping, sometimes silent. Over time, his students began noticing the change—he was calmer, more joyful, and inspired. Julian became known for "bringing peace into a room."

He says today, "My closet became my war room, and worship became my sword." Like Moses' tent of meeting, it was his holy ground in the middle of the mundane.

Journaling and Reflecting on God's Goodness

Writing is remembering. In Deuteronomy 6:12, Moses warned, *"Be careful not to forget the Lord who brought you out of Egypt."* We forget quickly. Journaling helps us track the footprints of God through our daily lives.

Keep a *Worship Journal* where you:

- ✓ Write down a daily Scripture that spoke to you.
- ✓ Record answered prayers—big and small.
- ✓ Pen your heart's response in worshipful language.
- ✓ Reflect on what you sense God is saying.

Faith Okoro – A Life Captured in Worship

Faith Okoro, a nurse from Lagos, Nigeria, began journaling after losing her younger sister to cancer. Initially, it was just grief on paper. But one day, she wrote out a Psalm in her own words—Psalm 23, rewritten from her valley of sorrow.

It became a healing act. She began every morning by writing one thing she was grateful for, one lyric she loved, and one verse that lifted her. Over months, the journal became a book—a private altar of God's faithfulness.

Today, she says, "When doubt knocks, I open my journal and remember who God is."

Practical Tool:
Personal Worship Diary Template

To help you establish your daily altar, use this simple format to record your daily worship journey:

WORSHIP DIARY – DAILY ALTAR ENTRY

Date:

Time Spent: (e.g., 20 mins)

Scripture for Today:

Key Verse Highlighted:

Worship Song Played/Sung:

Reflection: (What did you sense God saying today?)

Prayer Response:

Gratitude Note: (One thing you're thankful for today)

Spiritual Insight or Breakthrough Noticed:

Application: (What will you do differently today because of this time?)

Building this habit, day by day, may seem simple. But like Elijah's altar soaked in water, the fire falls on offerings made with intentionality and faith (1 Kings 18:33–38). Don't underestimate the quiet, consistent building of your personal altar. God sees, receives, and responds.

A Fire That Never Goes Out

In Leviticus 6:13, God commanded, *"The fire must be kept burning on the altar continuously; it must not go out."* That is the call for us today. Not flashy, not always emotional—but continuous.

When you build a daily altar, your heart becomes a dwelling place for God's presence. Worship ceases to be an event—it becomes your atmosphere, your resistance against darkness, your divine alignment.

You are not just a worshipper; you are the altar, the offering, and the song. And in that sacred offering, victory is forged, healing flows, and your spirit becomes a light in the thickest dark.

Chapter 12: Warfare in Worship – Corporate Settings

When Heaven Touches Earth Through Unified Sound

There is a distinct power that arises when believers come together in one spirit to exalt the name of the Lord. The Bible declares in Psalm 22:3 that God is enthroned on the praises of His people. Not one person—His people. This chapter explores how worship in *corporate settings*—whether in a local church, a home fellowship, or even on a citywide scale—becomes an instrument of divine warfare, spiritual alignment, and cultural reformation.

The church is not just a gathering place; it is a command center. And worship is not the warm-up to a sermon; it is often the battlefield where victories are won.

Leading Worship with Discernment

Worship leaders are not performers; they are spiritual midwives. Their responsibility is not to impress, but to listen—first to heaven, then to the room. Discernment is the gift that allows a worship leader to know what *God is doing* in the room and how to *partner with it.*

Biblical Example: Jehoshaphat's Appointed Singers

In 2 Chronicles 20, King Jehoshaphat faced a terrifying alliance of enemies. Instead of sending the army first, he appointed singers to go ahead, declaring: *"Give thanks to the LORD, for His love endures forever."* As they sang, the Lord set ambushes against their enemies.

They weren't just singing songs—they were discerning *heaven's strategy*. God wanted praise to precede the sword.

Mariah Chen – The Worship Leader Who Paused

Mariah Chen led worship at a growing urban church in Singapore. One Sunday morning, during a routine upbeat set, she suddenly felt the Holy Spirit stir her heart. She quietly stopped the team and whispered into the mic, "Let's wait on the Lord."

For two full minutes, the room was still. Then she gently played one chord on the keyboard and began to sing Psalm 46:10: *"Be still and know that I am God."* People began to weep. Some knelt. Others lifted their hands in silent awe.

After the service, a couple approached her. That morning, they had come ready to announce their separation. But in the stillness, they said, *"God reminded us of His covenant."* Worship saved a marriage.

Discernment isn't always loud. Sometimes, it's the ability to know when not to sing.

How Worship Can Transform a Church Culture

A church's culture is not defined by its walls or its branding, but by the atmosphere it cultivates. Worship, when rooted in Spirit and truth (John 4:23), becomes the foundation of a transformational culture. It invites vulnerability, faith, holiness, and hunger.

Biblical Example: The Upper Room

In Acts 1 and 2, 120 people waited in one place, united in prayer and praise. When the Holy Spirit came, their worship exploded into tongues, testimonies, and transformation. The culture of the early church was not formed by programs, but by a corporate encounter.

Pastor Isaiah and the Rural Revival

In a small church in Warangal, India, Pastor Isaiah's congregation had dwindled to twenty elderly members. There was apathy, gossip, and spiritual dryness. One evening, instead of preaching, Isaiah invited them to simply worship and thank God—for anything they could remember.

It began awkwardly. But slowly, voices lifted. One woman sang in her native tongue. Another clapped softly. Something shifted. Tears flowed. From that night on, they held 30-minute worship sessions before every service.

Within six months, families returned. Young people joined. Demonic oppressions were broken. One man who had been suicidal was baptized. Worship had shifted the spiritual climate—not just the mood of the room.

Worship redefines what is normal in a church. When God is glorified above programs, growth becomes the byproduct—not the goal.

Team Unity and Warfare Readiness

Worship teams are often the frontline warriors of a church's spiritual battle. But warfare requires unity. Discord within a team is not just a relational problem—it's a spiritual vulnerability.

Biblical Example: The Walls of Jericho

In Joshua 6, the priests blew trumpets and the people shouted *together*. The walls fell not because of volume, but because of unity in obedience. Imagine if the trumpeters had argued, or the people had shouted at the wrong time—the victory required synchronized trust in divine timing.

The Broken Strings and Mended Hearts

At Kingdom Life Church in Birmingham, England, the worship team had grown talented but fractured. Hidden offenses and subtle competition brewed. One Sunday, the electric guitar failed, the keys crashed, and the drummer didn't show up. The service was awkward, the worship felt "off."

That week, the team gathered not to rehearse, but to reconcile. They confessed. They prayed. They wept.

The next Sunday, with just a single acoustic guitar and raw voices, the atmosphere exploded with divine power. Healings took place during worship. Deliverance happened spontaneously.

Their takeaway? "God doesn't anoint performance. He anoints unity." Team readiness isn't just musical—it's spiritual and relational. Unity *prepares the battleground* for effective worship warfare.

Spiritual Mapping and Worship Strategy in Cities

Some cities carry spiritual strongholds—generational idolatry, poverty, addiction, or injustice. Spiritual mapping is the prophetic practice of identifying these forces and developing worship *strategies* to reclaim those territories for the Kingdom.

Biblical Example: Paul in Ephesus

In Acts 19, Paul's ministry in Ephesus was not merely preaching—it confronted regional demonic powers tied to Artemis worship. The entire city shifted because of consistent prayer, worship, and bold proclamation.

Zoe Makamba – A Map and a Mandate

Zoe Makamba, an intercessor in Nairobi, Kenya, sensed the Lord calling her to map out the spiritual history of her city. She researched the districts most affected by crime and generational curses. With a small team, she began hosting outdoor worship gatherings—not concerts, but spiritual acts of warfare.

They sang in local languages, declaring Christ as Lord over each neighborhood. Over two years, crime dropped in one district by 30%. Three local gang leaders gave their lives to Christ. Zoe says, *"We weren't just worshipping in the city—we were worshipping for the city."*

Worship, when done with prophetic insight, becomes territorial warfare. The sound of heaven invades the systems of earth.

Prayer + Worship: The Role of Intercession

Worship and intercession are the two lungs of a powerful church. One exhales praise, the other inhales heaven's burden. When they merge, the result is divine alignment and breakthrough.

Biblical Example: Paul and Silas in Prison

In Acts 16, Paul and Silas prayed *and* sang hymns. Their combined worship and intercession shook the prison, opened doors, and even led a jailer to Christ. Their voices in the dark released more than comfort—it released divine justice.

The Watchmen of Madison Street

A group of five intercessors in Detroit called themselves the Watchmen of Madison Street. Every Friday night, they gathered to pray and worship over their block—an area riddled with drug trafficking and violence.

They sang simple choruses, declared Scripture, and walked the streets as they worshipped. After eight months, a notorious drug house shut down. A local bar became a coffee shop. A Bible study was planted in an abandoned building.

Their intercession wasn't glamorous. But they were the *hidden furnace* fueling revival. Worship and prayer are not two ministries—they are one, united weapon in the hands of surrendered people.

Sound the Trumpet, Raise the Banner

Corporate worship is not a filler between announcements and sermons. It is the rallying cry of a heavenly army, preparing the way for God's glory to invade. It softens hearts, disrupts darkness, and redefines spiritual territory.

When a church learns to worship with discernment, cultivate unity in their teams, align with prophetic intercession, and intentionally engage their cities, worship becomes an unstoppable force. It doesn't just make people feel good—it makes the enemy tremble.

The call is clear: Raise a sound that shifts atmospheres. Lead not just with skill, but with reverence and insight. For when the people of God worship as one, with clean hands and pure hearts, the gates of hell cannot prevail.

Chapter 13: The Sound of Heaven – Unlocking Prophetic Worship

When Earth Echoes Heaven's Voice

In the spiritual realm, sound is not just a vibration—it is a *vehicle.* It carries the will, heart, and mind of God. It transports prophetic declarations, reveals divine mysteries, and unlocks the unseen. Worship that is prophetic does not simply retell what has already been sung; it *reveals what God is saying now.*

True prophetic worship is the sound of heaven breaking through the veil of time into human ears. It does not originate in rehearsals or planning meetings—it is born in intimacy, matured in obedience, and released in surrender.

Singing the Word – The Fusion of Scripture and Song

Singing the Word is one of the most powerful and safe ways to engage in prophetic worship. Scripture is already God-breathed, and when it is sung, it carries both truth and presence. The Psalms, which are essentially sung prayers, are filled with raw emotion, divine truths, prophetic decrees, and declarations of hope.

Biblical Example: Revelation 5:9–10

In Revelation 5:9–10, we witness a heavenly scene where the elders and living creatures sing a new song:

"You are worthy to take the scroll and to open its seals, because You were slain, and with Your blood

You purchased for God persons from every tribe and language and people and nation."

This song is not fiction—it is a *prophetic proclamation* of Christ's redemptive work and the gathering of a global church. It is truth, sung in real-time before the throne.

Luca and the Psalm of Deliverance

Luca Benitez, a youth pastor in Madrid, struggled for weeks with depression after the sudden death of his younger brother. He stopped leading worship and avoided public gatherings. One morning, while reading Psalm 40, the words *"He lifted me out of the slimy pit"* gripped his soul.

Unable to speak, he took his guitar and began to sing those verses aloud. The melody was raw, broken, and without rhythm—but it was full of life. As he continued singing the Psalm, something lifted. That Sunday, he sang it publicly, and others were deeply moved. Many wept—not because of a tune, but because they heard the Word alive and sung.

Singing Scripture bypasses the mind and enters the soul. It is God's voice clothed in melody.

Spontaneous Worship & Prophetic Flow – The River of the Spirit

Spontaneous worship is not planned; it is permitted. It is the moment when the worshipper, guided by the Holy Spirit, steps out of the structure and into the river of revelation. It may involve new songs, spontaneous lyrics, or unplanned prayers that emerge from deep communion with God.

Biblical Example: The Song of Mary

When Mary visited Elizabeth, the Holy Spirit stirred within her and she burst into spontaneous praise (Luke 1:46–55). Her song—*"My soul magnifies the*

Lord"—was not rehearsed. It was a spontaneous eruption of prophetic truth about the destiny of the child she carried.

Aaliyah Johnson – The Song of the Street

Aaliyah Johnson led worship at a small, inner-city church in New Orleans. One evening during a midweek service, as she ended a familiar worship song, a new melody welled up in her spirit. She hesitated, then began to sing: *"I walk through fire, but I do not burn; Your voice is louder than the storm."*

Tears filled her eyes. People in the room began to sing with her. One man in the back—Jerome, a recovering addict—collapsed to the floor sobbing. He said later, *"That line was my life. That was God speaking to me."*

Aaliyah had no idea what she was singing until the moment it left her lips. She was simply obedient to the flow. Spontaneous worship is God's poetry for the moment, written through willing vessels.

Worship in Tongues and Spiritual Language – Heaven's Undistracted Sound

There are moments when words fail. In those moments, the Spirit steps in—not with silence, but with sound. Singing or praying in tongues is not gibberish—it is heaven's language finding expression through earthly vessels.

Paul writes in 1 Corinthians 14:2:

"For anyone who speaks in a tongue does not speak to people but to God. Indeed, no one understands them; they utter mysteries by the Spirit."

When sung, tongues become melodies of mysteries. The human voice becomes a divine instrument, playing notes unknown to the mind but powerful in the spirit.

Biblical Example: The Upper Room Again

Acts 2 tells us that when the Holy Spirit fell, the disciples spoke in other tongues. The crowd heard them *declaring the wonders of God*. This was not confusion—it was a convergence of heaven and earth through language saturated in the Spirit.

Joram and the Unseen Battle

Joram Ndlovu, a worship leader from Cape Town, had a habit of praying in tongues privately but was hesitant to do so publicly. One Sunday, while ministering at a tent revival, he felt overwhelmed during a time of worship. He began singing in tongues softly over his microphone.

To his surprise, an elderly woman shouted from the crowd, "He's singing in Zulu!" Joram didn't speak Zulu. Yet the woman, who was on the verge of abandoning her faith, heard him declaring, *"The Lord fights your battle. You are not forgotten."*

Worship in tongues bypasses intellectual filters and releases *raw, divine utterance*. It is a mystery—but one filled with power, compassion, and deliverance.

Scripture and Foundations – Rooted in Truth, Led by the Spirit

Prophetic worship must never stand apart from the Word. It flows from the Word and returns to it, just as rain returns to the sea. Revelation 5:9–10 reminds us that worship in heaven is always Christ-centered, rooted in redemption, and aimed at eternal truths.

Paul balances spiritual fervor with biblical clarity in 1 Corinthians 14:26–33. He emphasizes that all things must be done *for edification* and *in order*. Prophetic worship should stir hearts, not confuse them. It must point to Jesus, not to the performer.

A prophetic song that carries no biblical anchor may move the emotions but will never move the heavens.

Echoing the Voice of the Throne Room

Prophetic worship is not a style—it is a stance. It is the posture of the worshipper who leans close to hear God's heartbeat and sings what they hear. Whether through Scripture, spontaneous flow, tongues, or melody, the sound of heaven is waiting to be released through your life.

The question is not whether God is speaking. The question is: Are we singing what we hear?

In the final vision of Revelation, every creature sings a new song to the Lamb. That is our destiny. But it is also our privilege—*right now*—to echo that sound here on earth.

Let your worship be more than music. Let it be a voice that prophesies, heals, and reveals the King.

Chapter 14: A Call to Nations – Worship as Global Intercession

"From the rising of the sun to its setting, the name of the Lord is to be praised." —Psalm 113:3

The song of the Lord is not meant to remain within the four walls of a sanctuary. From the beginning, God's intention for worship has always been global. In Psalm 67, the psalmist cries, "Let the nations be glad and sing for joy," a declaration not just of praise but of intercession—a longing for God's glory to cover the earth as the waters cover the sea.

In this hour, worship is being rediscovered not only as a sacred expression but as a weapon of global transformation. Worship is arising across continents—not just as performance or personal devotion, but as intercession for entire nations, shaking spiritual realms and aligning earthly realities with heaven's intentions.

This chapter is a prophetic trumpet call to worship teams, intercessors, missionaries, and ordinary believers alike: Your worship can move nations.

Worship Movements Changing Nations

In the early 2000s, something unusual began to stir across the earth: 24/7 prayer and worship movements began erupting in places like Kansas City (IHOPKC), Jerusalem (Succat Hallel), and Germany (The Burn). These were not orchestrated by human ambition but by divine invitation. The Holy Spirit was reclaiming worship as intercession.

Biblical Root: In Revelation 5:8, we see a heavenly picture—golden bowls full of incense, which are *the prayers of the saints*, mingled with *harp and song*. Worship and intercession are eternally entwined. What the worship movements have rediscovered is that singing is a form of warfare, and music can shape history when saturated with the presence of God.

Case Example: IHOPKC (International House of Prayer – Kansas City)

24/7 worship and prayer have been lifted from Kansas City to heaven without interruption since September 19, 1999. What began with a few people in a small trailer became a global model, inspiring prayer rooms from Uganda to Ukraine. The result? Missionaries launched, cities transformed, and regions awakened.

But the true miracle isn't in the size of the movement—it's in its consistency. The priests never leave the altar. And that, more than anything, shifts atmospheres over nations.

Apostolic Worship and Spiritual Territories

Worship is not just musical—it is apostolic. Apostolic worship doesn't just sing songs about God; it releases His *government* into regions. In 2 Chronicles 20, when Judah faced annihilation, they didn't send an army—they sent *worshippers*. As they sang, *"Give thanks to the Lord, for His love endures forever,"* God set ambushes against their enemies. Worship took spiritual territory.

Character Story: Pastor Elijah Varghese – Kerala, India

In a small fishing village on the coast of Kerala, a quiet man named Elijah Varghese received a vision during prayer. In it, he saw drums and harps circling the borders of his state and a wave of light crashing over dark places. He understood it as a call to raise *worship intercessors*.

Elijah trained young fishermen to sing the Word and pray in the Spirit. They met under coconut trees, lifting up psalms in Malayalam and English. Over time, reports of reduced alcoholism, healing miracles, and salvations began to pour in. One local temple priest publicly testified that "the song of these Christians carries something I cannot understand but cannot resist."

Elijah never called himself an apostle, but heaven did. His worship rewrote the spiritual script of an entire coastal district.

Worship Teams as Frontline Warriors

Worship teams are not background performers; they are the tip of the spear in spiritual warfare. In times of revival and resistance, worship teams carry the first sound into enemy territory. The book of Judges tells us that Judah—the tribe of *praise*—was sent first into battle (Judges 1:2). The same strategy remains in the Spirit.

Character Story: Miriam Park – Seoul, South Korea

Miriam Park led a young worship team at a university in Seoul. Known for her purity of heart and Spirit-led singing, she began teaching her team to not just rehearse songs, but to intercede for their city before each practice.

One night during rehearsal, the Spirit fell heavily. One of the musicians began to sing in tongues while another received a vision of North Korea opening its doors. They sang a spontaneous song over North Korea—declaring peace, gospel access, and unity.

Two weeks later, the headlines broke: a small delegation from North Korea had crossed into the South for cultural peace talks—the first in over a decade. Miriam and her team realized that what seemed like a small worship night was actually a heavenly operation.

Spiritual Mapping and Intercessory Worship

Some worship teams are called to not just sing in churches but to *map the spiritual landscape* of cities. Spiritual mapping involves identifying strongholds, praying over locations, and releasing strategic worship to displace principalities.

Character Story: Musa Otieno – Nairobi, Kenya

Musa was a street drummer in Nairobi turned worship leader after a radical conversion. With little formal education but deep spiritual insight, Musa began walking the streets of Nairobi at dawn with his team, playing shofars and singing worship over key buildings—parliament, schools, hospitals, and red-light districts.

He called it "taking the song where the suffering is." As they worshiped, crime rates dropped in some of the most violent neighborhoods, and reports of peace and restoration began surfacing. What was once a local experiment became a movement. Today, Musa leads citywide worship nights across Kenya—ushering in waves of deliverance and revival.

A New Sound Rising: Testimonies from Nations

Bali: "From Temples to Thrones"

In one of the cities known for deep-rooted idolatry, a young believer named Sneha Joshi felt compelled to sing worship songs in the local language near a river. Every evening, amidst temple bells and chants, she would quietly sing Scriptures. Over months, several widows of other faith began to sit near her, drawn to "the peace in her voice." One of them, a woman named Meera, encountered Jesus in a dream—after hearing Sneha sing Psalm 23 repeatedly.

Iran: "Worship Behind the Walls"

Ali Reza, once a devout follower of Islam, began leading underground house churches in Tehran. Without instruments, he and his wife would whisper songs of worship over families. Even in the silence, they felt angelic presence. One night, while they worshipped in hushed tones, a loud noise like a rushing wind filled the room. A paralyzed woman was instantly healed. That house church now multiplies weekly—even under persecution. Worship is unstoppable.

Africa: "The Drums That Broke Witchcraft"

In a tribal village in Ghana, a team of youth worshippers known as *The Fire Sound* marched around the village every Friday night singing songs to Jesus. Elders mocked them until a well-known sorcerer fell to the ground as they passed and cried, "The fire is burning me!" That man later gave his life to Christ. Today, that village has three churches where there was once only fear.

United States: "Silicon Valley Awakens"

A worship leader named Jordan Miles felt called to host worship in downtown San Jose, in front of tech company headquarters. He and his team sang prophetic songs about purpose, identity, and destiny. Employees began joining, some crying, some curious. It grew into a "worship lunch break" attended by over 300 weekly. Several engineers testified that the "music opened something they didn't know they had been missing."

The Earth Will Be Filled

The sound of intercession through worship is not a fad—it is the heartbeat of heaven. The Lamb is worthy, and the nations are His inheritance. Worship teams are no longer confined to platforms. They are soldiers in sanctuaries, evangelists with microphones, and watchmen on walls.

In Revelation 7:9–10, John sees a vision of all tribes, nations, and tongues standing before the throne *worshiping the Lamb*. That is the final picture of history—and our worship today is preparing the earth for that scene.

This chapter is not just a history—it is a commissioning.

Will you raise your voice for your nation?

Will you train your team to pray with their instruments?

Will you be part of the sound that prepares the way for the King?

SECTION V:
Action Plan – Becoming a Worshipper Who Wages War

Chapter 15:
21-Day Worship Warrior Challenge

"Blessed be the LORD, my Rock, who trains my hands for war and my fingers for battle." —Psalm 144:1

Worship is not passive. It's not background music for devotionals. It's a declaration of God's kingship, a tearing down of strongholds, and a prophetic act of war. But becoming a *worshipper who wages war* doesn't happen by accident. It's a journey of surrender, intimacy, and proclamation.

This 21-day challenge is a training ground. It is meant to rewire your spiritual reflexes so that worship becomes your first weapon in every battle.

WEEK 1: Surrender & Consecration

Before you can lift your hands in warfare, they must be clean. Worship that breaks through the heavens begins with hearts that are fully yielded. This first week is about consecration—bringing every idol, distraction, and false comfort to the altar and laying it down.

- ✓ Daily Focus: Laying Down Idols
- ✓ Scripture Foundation: *"Those who cling to worthless idols turn away from God's love for them." – Jonah 2:8*

Character Story: Leah Mensah – Ghana

Leah was a talented worship singer in her local church in Accra. Though gifted, her heart longed more for Instagram validation than God's affirmation. One night during worship, she sensed the Lord whisper, *"Will you lay down your platform for My presence?"*

Convicted, Leah went silent for a week. No music. No social media. No stage. During that fasted time, she journaled daily, weeping over the idols she had unknowingly built. By day five, her heart felt light, her song changed, and the anointing on her voice tripled. What once sounded polished now carried power.

Worship Song Suggestions (Daily):

- ✓ “Refiner” – Maverick City Music
- ✓ “Heart of Worship” – Matt Redman
- ✓ “More Than Anything” – Lamar Campbell

Journal Prompt Examples (Daily):

- ✓ “Lord, what have I held onto more tightly than You?”
- ✓ “What part of me resists surrender?”
- ✓ “Is there anything I’ve been afraid to give You control of?”

Each day ends in worship—not asking, but adoring. In surrender, your worship becomes pure. Consecration clears the battlefield.

WEEK 2: Intimacy & Intercession

Worship isn’t a monologue; it’s a divine dialogue. Week 2 calls you to lean into the heartbeat of God through His names, His Word, and personal communion. Here, you begin to sing what He says, not just what you feel.

- ✓ Daily Focus: Declaring God's Names, Praying the Word
- ✓ Scripture Foundation: “The name of the Lord is a strong tower; the righteous run to it and are safe.” – *Proverbs 18:10*
- ✓ Each day, you choose one name of God and worship from that revelation—Jehovah Rapha, El Roi, Adonai, El Shaddai, Yahweh Nissi, and more. You also speak out Scripture as prayer.

Character Story: Jordan Peña – New Mexico, USA

Jordan, a former addict turned worship leader, struggled with anxiety attacks that returned even after his salvation. One night, overwhelmed with fear, he felt paralyzed during a worship set. In desperation, he opened to Psalm 91 and began *declaring it aloud as a song*. Something shifted.

From that night, Jordan began writing worship songs directly from the Psalms. His personal battles became public weapons. Today, those songs are sung in recovery centers across the southwest. He found that praying and singing the Word made him unshakable.

Daily Action Steps & Faith Activations:

- ✓ Meditate on a new name of God each day (e.g., Jehovah Jireh – The Lord Who Provides).
- ✓ Write a one-line prayer based on that name and sing it.
- ✓ Declare Scripture aloud in your room as a prophetic act.

Worship Song Suggestions:

- ✓ "Way Maker" – Sinach
- ✓ "Great Are You Lord" – All Sons & Daughters
- ✓ "The Names of God" – Laurell Hubick

Journal Prompt Examples (Daily):

- ✓ "What name of God speaks to my current battle?"
- ✓ "Where have I seen God show up as [Name] in my life?"
- ✓ "What Scripture do I need to turn into a song today?"

WEEK 3: Proclamation & Praise in Battle

This final week is your battleground. The idols are laid down. Your heart is intimate with the Father. Now, your voice becomes a sword. Worship isn't reactive—it's offensive. You will declare before the breakthrough. You will praise before the walls fall.

- ✓ Daily Focus: Warfare Declarations, Prophetic Praise
- ✓ Scripture Foundation: "Let the high praises of God be in their mouths, and a double-edged sword in their hands." – *Psalm 149:6*

Character Story: Ayaka Nakamura – Osaka, Japan

Ayaka was part of a house church hidden in a city where Christianity was still taboo. One morning, as government tension escalated, her community was instructed to "cease all spiritual gatherings." Instead of fear, Ayaka gathered a few close friends and began singing softly in her living room.

As they praised, she began to prophetically declare, *"The God of Angel Armies is standing guard over Osaka!"* The next day, the crackdown was lifted. No one could explain it. But Ayaka knew: *praise had cleared the air.*

Worship Action Steps (Daily):

- ✓ Write your own declaration song over your city.
- ✓ Use your phone to record yourself singing a spontaneous praise.
- ✓ Walk your neighborhood while singing praises aloud (or softly if needed).
- ✓ Engage in 7-minute "victory praise" dances like Miriam did in Exodus 15.

Worship Song Suggestions:

- ✓ "Surrounded (This is How I Fight My Battles)" – Upper Room

- ✓ "Raise a Hallelujah" – Bethel Music
- ✓ "Victor's Crown" – Darlene Zschech

Final Commissioning Journal Prompts (Last Day):

- ✓ "What did God build in me during these 21 days?"
- ✓ "What battle has shifted through my worship?"
- ✓ "Where is God sending me next to carry this sound?"

Prayer of Commissioning:

Father, I offer my voice, my hands, and my heart to You. Make me a worshipper who wars in the Spirit. Let every song I sing release truth into darkness. Let my feet carry praise into unreached places. Train me to worship when I feel weak, to declare when I see nothing, and to dance even in the valley. In Jesus' name, amen.

Closing Words

These 21 days will mark a shift—not just in your schedule, but in your spirit. You are not emerging as a singer but as a warrior of worship. The earth is groaning for sons and daughters who will sing what heaven is saying. You are now one of them.

So go. Open your mouth. Lift your hands. March around your Jericho. And don't stop until the walls fall.

Chapter 16:
Building an Altar in Your Home

"As for me and my house, we will serve the Lord." — Joshua 24:15

In the days of Abraham, Isaac, and Jacob, altars were physical spaces—stones stacked in sacred memory, places where men met with God and God revealed Himself to men. Today, under the new covenant, the altar is the heart—but it must still be built, tended, and offered daily, especially in the home.

We cannot expect revival in our cities if there is no worship in our living rooms. The home altar is where nations are discipled, where sons and daughters are shaped, and where the glory of God first rests before it can flood the streets.

This chapter is a call to rebuild what many families have let crumble—the daily family altar of worship.

Creating a Sacred Space

Not every home has a spare room for prayer, but every home can make space for God. What matters most is not square footage but sacred intentionality.

Biblical Anchor

In 2 Kings 4, the Shunammite woman prepared a small upper room for Elisha, the prophet of God. It contained just a bed, a table, a chair, and a lampstand. Yet because she made room for God's presence, her home became the site of a miracle—the resurrection of her son.

Creating a sacred space doesn't require extravagance. It requires recognition: *God must have a place in this house.*

Character Story: Jerome & Lianne Koh — Singapore

Jerome, a software engineer, and his wife Lianne, a part-time music teacher, were raising three children in a tiny two-bedroom flat in Singapore. Their home was loud, cluttered, and often chaotic. After a sermon on making room for God, they cleared a corner near their dining table and placed a simple shelf with a Bible, a candle, and a small wooden cross their daughter had made in Sunday school.

That corner became their altar.

Every morning at 6:30 AM, before breakfast and work, Jerome played a worship instrumental, and the family would pray or read a Psalm together. It was never long—sometimes just 10 minutes—but over time, the peace of God seemed to linger even in the busiest mornings.

One evening, their 9-year-old son Ethan paused while playing with Legos and whispered, *"Can I go to the altar? I feel like talking to God."* Lianne wept silently. God was no longer a guest. He was at home in their home.

Training Your Children in Worship

One of the most sacred responsibilities given to parents is to disciple their children in the way of the Lord. Worship is not just taught—it's caught. Children watch what we prioritize. If our homes are filled with television noise, sports stats, or endless scrolling, they will learn distraction. If our homes are filled with praise and prayer, they will learn devotion.

Biblical Anchor

In Deuteronomy 6:6–7, the Lord commands,

"These commandments that I give you today are to be on your hearts. Impress them on your children.

Talk about them when you sit at home and when you walk along the road..."

God never intended for spiritual instruction to be confined to the temple or church building. The home was always meant to be the first sanctuary.

Character Story: Anita Rodriguez – Bogotá, Colombia

Anita, a single mother of two, had recently recommitted her life to Christ after years of bitterness. Her daughter Lucia, age 14, and son Mateo, age 10, were indifferent to church.

Instead of forcing them into religious behavior, Anita began by simply playing soft worship music while cooking. She started journaling praises to God at the kitchen table, often praying aloud as she did.

One night, Lucia came in quietly and said, *"I wrote a poem. Can I read it to God like you do?"* It wasn't long before Mateo followed, bringing his drumsticks to keep rhythm while Anita sang Psalms. Their worship altar wasn't neat or formal—but it was alive.

Worshipping as a Family or Household

Family worship is not meant to be a performance or a duty. It is an invitation to communion. In worship, we align together not just as family members, but as priests before God.

It may feel awkward at first. Some members may be resistant. The key is consistency, grace, and the understanding that worship transforms hearts in time.

Biblical Anchor

In Acts 10, we meet Cornelius, a Roman centurion described as "a devout man who feared God with all his household." Because of his home's reverence, an angel visited, Peter was sent, and his entire family was filled with the Holy Spirit. One man's home altar brought a divine visitation that birthed Gentile revival.

Character Story: David & Priya Menon – Kerala, India

David and Priya were the first Christians in their Hindu family line. After their baptism, they began praying each night with their two daughters, aged 11 and 7. It started with simple choruses in Malayalam, followed by Scripture reading and prayer.

Within three months, their older daughter began praying for her grandparents' salvation. One evening, while the family worshipped, the grandfather—once hostile—stood at the door, weeping. "Your singing reminds me of something I lost long ago," he whispered. That night, he asked for prayer.

A simple family altar turned a household enemy into a seeker of Christ.

Sample Family Worship Guide

This is not a rigid program, but a suggested rhythm. Adjust for your family's age range, time availability, and flow.

Daily Family Worship (15–20 minutes)

Call to Worship (1–2 minutes)

Play soft worship. Say aloud: "This house belongs to the Lord."

Worship Song (3–5 minutes)

Choose a familiar song or teach a new one weekly. Encourage everyone to sing along or clap.

Scripture Reading (5 minutes)

Read a Psalm or short passage. Invite each person to share what one verse means to them.

Prayer Time (5–10 minutes)

Rotate prayer leadership among family members. Each person can thank God, pray for one another, and intercede for others.
Blessing (1 minute)
Close with a blessing over each child: *"The Lord bless you and keep you…"* (Numbers 6:24–26)

The House That Hosts God
Worship is not confined to cathedrals. The most powerful revivals often begin around dinner tables, in bedtime songs, and whispered morning prayers. A home that worships becomes a gate of heaven.
God is looking for families like Abraham's, like Cornelius's, like the Menons in Kerala and the Rodriguez family in Bogotá—those who will say, "We will build Him an altar right here."
You don't need stained glass or a seminary degree. You need hunger. You need heart. And you need to say, "Yes, Lord—start with us."

Family Worship Kit- A Sample

Introduction

This Family Worship Kit is designed to help families establish a daily rhythm of worship, prayer, and Scripture reflection together. It includes suggested songs, memory verses, journaling prompts, and a 7-day devotional guide.

Song Suggestions

Use simple, easily singable songs that can involve children and adults alike. Songs can be sung a cappella or with simple instruments like a keyboard or guitar.

Sample Songs:

1. *This Is The Day That The Lord Has Made*
2. *He's Got The Whole World In His Hands*
3. *Goodness of God*
4. *Way Maker*
5. *What A Beautiful Name*

Memory Verses

Day 1: Joshua 24:15 – *'As for me and my house, we will serve the Lord.'*

Day 2: Psalm 100:4 – *'Enter His gates with thanksgiving and His courts with praise.'*

Day 3: Proverbs 3:5 – *'Trust in the Lord with all your heart and lean not on your own understanding.'*

Day 4: Psalm 119:105 – *'Your word is a lamp to my feet and a light for my path.'*

Day 5: Matthew 5:14 – *'You are the light of the world.'*

Day 6: Romans 12:1 – *'Offer your bodies as a living sacrifice, holy and pleasing to God.'*

Day 7: Philippians 4:6 – *'Do not be anxious about anything, but in everything, by prayer and petition, with thanksgiving, present your requests to God.'*

Journaling Template

Each day, use the following questions to reflect as a family or individually:

1. *What did I learn about God today?*
2. *What am I thankful for today?*
3. *Is there anything I need to ask forgiveness for?*
4. *How can I show God's love to others today?*
5. *What verse stood out to me and why?*

Space for Response:

____

____

____

7-Day Devotional Plan

Day 1: Consecrate Your Home

- ✓ Read: Joshua 24:15
- ✓ Reflect: What does it mean for your home to serve the Lord?
- ✓ Prayer: Dedicate your family and space to God's glory.

Day 2: Praise As A Weapon

- ✓ Read: Psalm 149:6
- ✓ Reflect: How can praise silence fear?
- ✓ Activity: Sing a song of victory together.

Day 3: Listening to God

- ✓ Read: 1 Samuel 3:10
- ✓ Reflect: Practice listening in silence after prayer.
- ✓ Activity: Share if anyone sensed God speaking.

Day 4: Trusting God Daily

- ✓ Read: Proverbs 3:5-6
- ✓ Reflect: Share one area where you need to trust God more.
- ✓ Prayer: Ask for God's guidance.

Day 5: Worship Through Service

- ✓ Read: Matthew 25:40
- ✓ Reflect: Plan one act of kindness as a family.
- ✓ Activity: Do it together.

Day 6: Family Forgiveness

- ✓ Read: Colossians 3:13
- ✓ Reflect: Is there anyone in the family who needs to forgive or ask for forgiveness?
- ✓ Prayer: Pray a prayer of healing.

Day 7: Thanksgiving Celebration

- ✓ Read: 1 Thessalonians 5:18
- ✓ Reflect: Share what you're most thankful for this week.
- ✓ Activity: Write a family gratitude letter to God.

Chapter 17:
Final Charge – Worshippers Will Win

"Let everything that has breath praise the Lord. Praise the Lord." – Psalm 150:6

In the closing moments of a war, there is a call—a clarion cry—not just to survive, but to finish well. In the spiritual realm, that cry is worship. It is not a soft song for the weary; it is a victorious shout, the sound of a people who have seen the faithfulness of God in the fire, in the storm, and on the mountaintop. This is the final charge to every reader, every believer, every would-be warrior: Worshippers will win. Always.

A Lasting Legacy of Sound

Worship leaves behind something that weapons never can: a legacy of sound that echoes in the heavens long after battles are over. From the beginning, sound has shaped creation. God spoke the world into being (Genesis 1), and the heavens have been resounding with that rhythm ever since.

The legacy of worship is seen in King David, who wrote songs that became sacred scripture. David did not merely defeat Goliath with a sling; he defeated generations of fear by lifting songs that still stir courage centuries later. In his Psalms, he cried, lamented, rejoiced, and warred. Long after his death, his words still remind us that worship is both intimacy and artillery in the hands of the faithful.

Similarly, Mary of Bethany left a legacy when she broke her alabaster jar at Jesus' feet. Jesus declared, "Wherever this gospel is preached throughout the world, what she has done will also be told, in memory of her" (Matthew 26:13). It was an act of worship so potent that it marked eternity. She didn't preach, she didn't teach—she worshipped.

Leah's Legacy

Leah Mathews, a widow in her sixties, lived quietly in a coastal village in Kerala, India. She had lost her husband early, had no children, and lived with physical pain due to arthritis. And yet, every dawn she would play her old harmonium and sing psalms to the Lord. She would weep, not in sorrow, but in surrender. Those who walked past her little home would pause, strangely drawn by the peace that hovered there.

Years later, a young man named Reuben, who had grown up hearing her worship through the window, became a missionary to war-torn Sudan. When asked what inspired his strength, he said, "It was the sound of a broken woman who never let her pain be louder than her praise."

Worshipers like Leah leave behind more than memories—they leave altars others can build on.

The Eternal Destiny of Worship

Scripture shows us that worship isn't just a part of our Christian life—it is our eternal vocation. In Revelation 5:11–14, John sees a vision of the throne room of God, where thousands upon thousands of angels and every creature in heaven and on earth cry out in worship.

There will be no sermons in heaven. No more evangelistic crusades. No more miracles to be performed. But worship? Worship remains.

Lucifer was once the appointed cherub, filled with music, created to reflect the glory of God (Ezekiel 28:13–15). When pride entered his heart, he sought worship for himself and was cast down. But heaven's void was not left empty. God raised up us—the redeemed—to fill the atmosphere with worship.

You and I were not created for performance, productivity, or applause. We were created to behold God and give Him glory forever.

Kojo's Vision

Kojo was a teenage refugee in Ghana who had lost both his parents to civil conflict. Traumatized and silent for months, he wandered into a small missionary-led school where worship music played daily. One evening, during a simple worship gathering, Kojo began to cry uncontrollably. That night, he had a vision: he saw Jesus in white, surrounded by light and sound, singing over him.

Kojo later became a worship leader—not a famous one—but one who sang with such depth that demons fled from the room. His gift wasn't vocal. It was **prophetic intimacy** born from the ashes of grief. When asked what he believed his calling was, he answered, "To join the sound that never stops in heaven."

Worship aligns us with the reality of eternity. It prepares us to live not just for God, but with God, in unbroken communion.

Becoming a Worship Warrior Wherever You Go

You don't have to stand on a platform to be a worshipper. You don't need instruments, lights, or even a congregation. Worship warriors are mobile tabernacles, carrying the presence of God wherever they go.

Whether you are an accountant balancing numbers, a mother raising children, a bus driver navigating traffic, or a student preparing for exams—your worship is your warfare. It sanctifies the ordinary. It silences the lies. It sets the atmosphere.

Romans 12:1 urges us to present our bodies as "living sacrifices, holy and acceptable to God—this is your spiritual act of worship." This means your thoughts, your emotions, your labor, your laughter, your silence—they can all be worship.

Danielle at the Station

Danielle Rhodes was a train station janitor in a bustling city in the UK. Most people didn't notice her. But Danielle had a secret: she prayed over every bench she cleaned, sang softly as she mopped the floor, and blessed every traveler in her heart.

One day, a businessman collapsed in front of her. As people panicked, Danielle laid hands and prayed over him, quietly singing a chorus she often sang during her shift. When paramedics arrived, the man regained consciousness. Later, he would say, "I don't know what happened, but I felt peace come over me the moment she touched me."

Worship warriors don't just sing. They shift atmospheres. They bring Kingdom presence into enemy territory without fear.

The Final Trumpet

The final charge to you, dear reader, is simple: Keep singing. Keep worshipping. Keep building altars. When the war grows darker, your worship must grow louder—not in volume, but in clarity, in conviction, in truth.

Let your life release a sound that heaven recognizes, hell fears, and the earth is drawn to. Your victory doesn't come from your strength, strategy, or perfection. It comes from your surrender.

Because in the end, the worshippers will win.

Prayer of Commissioning:
Father, I offer myself as a living sacrifice. Let my life be an altar and my heart a sanctuary. Teach my hands to war with praise, my voice to echo heaven's sound, and my feet to walk in Your authority. Let worship not be something I do, but who I am. Anoint me to stand, to sing, to declare, and to shift the atmosphere—until the whole earth is filled with Your glory. In Jesus' Name. Amen.

Appendix:
25 Scriptures on Worship in Warfare

1. *Exodus 15:2 – The Lord is my strength and my song; he has given me victory.*
2. *Deuteronomy 20:4 – For the Lord your God is the one who goes with you to fight for you against your enemies to give you victory.*
3. *Joshua 6:20 – When the trumpets sounded, the army shouted… the wall collapsed.*
4. *1 Samuel 17:47 – The battle is the Lord's, and he will give all of you into our hands.*
5. *2 Samuel 22:4 – I called to the Lord, who is worthy of praise, and have been saved from my enemies.*
6. *2 Chronicles 20:22 – As they began to sing and praise, the Lord set ambushes against the men of Ammon...*
7. *Nehemiah 8:10 – The joy of the Lord is your strength.*
8. *Psalm 18:3 – I called to the Lord, who is worthy of praise, and I have been saved from my enemies.*
9. *Psalm 27:6 – Then my head will be exalted above the enemies who surround me... I will sing and make music to the Lord.*
10. *Psalm 68:1 – May God arise, may his enemies be scattered; may his foes flee before him.*
11. *Psalm 149:6 – May the praise of God be in their mouths and a double-edged sword in their hands...*

12. *Psalm 68:1 – "Let God arise, let His enemies be scattered; let those who hate Him flee before Him."*
13. *Psalm 91:1 – "He who dwells in the secret place of the Most High shall abide under the shadow of the Almighty."*
14. *Psalm 144:1 – "Blessed be the Lord my Rock, who trains my hands for war, and my fingers for battle."*
15. *Isaiah 30:32 – "Every stroke the Lord lays on them with his punishing club will be to the music of timbrels and harps."*
16. *Isaiah 61:3 – "To give them the garment of praise for the spirit of heaviness…"*
17. *Habakkuk 3:19 – "The Sovereign Lord is my strength; He makes my feet like the feet of a deer…"*
18. *Zephaniah 3:17 – "The Lord your God is with you… He will rejoice over you with singing."*
19. *2 Corinthians 10:4 – "The weapons of our warfare are not carnal but mighty in God…"*
20. *Revelation 19:6 – "Then I heard what sounded like a great multitude, like the roar of rushing waters…"*
21. *Psalm 24:8 – "Who is this King of glory? The Lord strong and mighty, the Lord mighty in battle."*
22. *Proverbs 18:10 – "The name of the Lord is a strong tower…"*
23. *Romans 8:37 – "In all these things we are more than conquerors through Him who loved us."*
24. *James 5:13 – "Is anyone among you in trouble? Let them pray. Is anyone happy? Let them sing songs of praise."*

25. *Revelation 14:2 – "And I heard a sound from heaven like the roar of rushing waters…"*

About the Author
'GERARD ASSEY'

Gerard Assey is a Graduate in Economics, a PGD in Management (HRD) and holds a Doctorate in Leadership. Gerard holds several International Qualifications in Sales, Debt Collection, Training & Teaching, and is a 'Fellow' of the prestigious 'Institute of Sales & Marketing Management'-UK, a Certified NLP Practitioner, a 'Certified Trainer', an 'Accredited Management Teacher-Behavioral Sciences', a 'Certified Competency Facilitator', a 'Certified Management Consultant'- (the International credentials of a professional management consultant, awarded in accordance with global standards of the ICMCI); and a Certification from the University of Michigan in 'Successful Negotiation: Essential Strategies and Skills'

He is also a Member of the 'National Association of Sales Professionals' backed with several years experience in varied industries, both in India and Overseas. He also holds an 'Etiquette Consultant' Certification from the USA (by Sue Fox, Author of Best Seller: 'Business Etiquette for Dummies'. She has trained some of the top celebrities' world over). He was also a recipient of a scholarship for extensive training in Japan on 'Corporate Management for India'.

Gerard Assey is 'Founder & Chief Corporate Trainer' of the Group: '**Citius, Altius, Fortius Unlimited**'- an organization that **celebrated 20 years of Glorious Service** in 2021, focusing on 3 Core Competencies:

People. Performance. Profit; in functional areas of Sales & Marketing, HR & Organizational Development, covering Recruitment, Training & Consultancy!

Having managed organizations with large Sales Forces in India & Overseas, his specialization cover extensive areas of Sales Training (All levels - Presentation, Negotiation, Key/ Strategic Accounts Management & Managerial Skills for all sectors), Bid Proposal/ Capture Planning/ Management Trainings, Retail Sales, Customer Service & Customer Retention Programs, Training for Prevention & Collection of Debt, Self & Personal Development Programs (Time Management, Teamwork & Team Building, Business Etiquette & Personal Grooming, Leadership & Managerial Skills, People Management Skills, Train-the-Trainer etc), including preparation of Custom-designed Business Manuals for Internal (HR, Induction, and Sales etc) & External use (Instruction, User Manuals).

Gerard has successfully conducted over 6450 Trainings & Workshops (as of May '25) all across India, Middle East, Africa, Europe & S.E. Asia. Besides public programs conducted regularly, both in India & Overseas, he has some of the top names as clients whom he services from Single Owners to large Public & Government undertakings, covering all sectors, for their in-house needs.

His website: www.CollectionSkills.com is the only one in this part of the world to be featured in the 'Collections & Credit Risk Magazine-USA' under 'Who's Who in Training' and ranks TOP, along with other websites listed below on most search engines.

Gerard is author of 193 books already (May 2025), all the books being available on all online platforms and outlets as E-books and Paperbacks

A few of our business related books:

1. Bite-sized Bits on Commonsense Management
2. Heart to Heart on Life's Principles'
3. How to become a Successful Manager
4. The Sales Professionals' Master Workbook of S.Y.S.T.E.M.S
5. The Professional Business Email Etiquette Handbook & Guide
6. The Professional Business Video-Conferencing Etiquette Handbook & Guide
7. Professional Presentation Skills
8. Exceptional Customer Service
9. Professional Tele-Marketing Skills
10. Professional Debt Collection Skills
11. The G.R.E.A.T. Sales & Service Workbook
12. Sales Training Advantage for Results (*The Ultimate Sales Training Manual to enable you stand out as a S.T.A.R.*)
13. CEO Daily Planner & Organizer
14. The Sales Professionals' Master Daily Planner
15. The Professional Debt Collector's Master Daily Planner
16. My Daily Planner & Organizer
17. MY EMERGENCY INFORMATION RECORD (Family Emergency & Peace of Mind Planner)
18. The Ultimate Therapist & Counselors Planner and Organizer
19. Building an Ethical Workplace
20. Managing Relationships at Work
21. Managing Business Meetings Effectively
22. Effective Delegation Skills
23. Goal Setting for Success
24. B2B Selling by Email
25. Professional Business Etiquette & Grooming
26. Dining Etiquette & Table Manners
27. Effective Networking Skills
28. Grooming, Etiquette & Manners for Teens, Young Adults & Future Leaders
29. Inter-Personal Skills
30. Get Ready, Get Hired!
31. Selling in a Recession
32. Effective Receivables Management in an Economic Downturn!
33. Real Estate & Property Sales Training
34. Credit Sales & Accounts Receivable Management

35. Selling Skills for Real Estate & Property Advisors
36. Take G.R.E.A.T. C.A.R.E!
37. Spa, Salon & Health Club Selling Skills
38. Selling Travel, Holiday & MICE Services
39. Selling Skills for Spa's, Salons & Health Clubs
40. Retailing in Salons & Spas
41. Selling Holiday, Vacation, Tours & Packages
42. The Power of Sales Referrals
43. Selling Luxury
44. Technical Selling Skills
45. Financial Advisors Sales Training
46. Dealing with Burnout at Work Monopolize Your Markets
47. Selling to Affluent Customers
48. Growing up with Grace
49. Financial Selling Skills
50. *The Effective Manager's Guide: Key Skills to Thrive*
51. From Aspiring to Inspiring: A Guide for New Managers on the Rise
52. The Power of Focus
53. Selling with Integrity: Sell Like Jesus The Perfect Role Model!
54. 31 Habits of Champions: Your 31-Day Journey to Greatness
55. Rejecting Grasshopper Talk: From Grasshopper to Giant-Killer-*Defeating Giants Daily!*
56. Navigate the AI-Powered Future of Bid & Proposals: Up-Skill to Stay Relevant with Alternative Career Paths & Opportunities
57. Hiring Sales Winners
58. Present with Impact
59. Success Unlocked: *Breaking Free from Habits that Hold You Back*
60. Complaints to Cheers, Feedback to Gold: Mastering Complaints Management
61. Thriving Together: *Cultivating Diversity, Equity, and Inclusion*
62. Coaching Skills for Sales Managers
63. Soaring to Success in Business & Leadership: Swifter, Higher, Stronger!
64. From Classroom to Podium: A Student's Guide to Powerful Public Speaking & Presentation Skills
65. Developing Self-Discipline
66. The CEO's 31-Day Power Plan: Unlocking Success through Essential Traits

67. Credibility Matters
68. A Winning Attitude
69. Bid & Proposal Management Using AI
70. Sales Forecasting: A Practical & Proven Guide to Strategic Sales Forecasting
71. Elevate & Energize: *50 Dynamic & Fun Activities for Peak Workplace Morale*
72. 'Sales SOS! Sales on Fire! *30 Days to Conquer Chaos & the Nightmares of Success!'*
73. Mastering Sales Managerial Skills: *Building High-Performing Teams & Driving Exceptional Results*
74. Eagle-Eyed Leadership: Unleashing the Power of 31 Lessons from Eagles
75. The Ultimate Employee Training Guide: *Training Today, Leading Tomorrow*
76. Being More Accountable at Work
77. Creating a Culture of Continuous Improvement
78. Effective Questioning & Listening Skills
79. The Power of Value Selling
80. The Growth Mindset
81. Mastering Professional Help Desk Skills
82. The Power to Lead with Empathy
83. Being Prepared: The Key to Unlocking Success
84. Youthful Spark-Youth Energizers, Activities and Games-Igniting the Fun in Youth
85. Ignite your Motivation for Success
86. Elevate Your Executive Presence: *Your Roadmap to Executive Excellence*
87. Smart Decisions: *Mastering Problem Solving with Strategic Solutions for Business Success*
88. Strategic Planning: *Developing and Implementing Strategic Plans to Achieve Long-Term Business Goals*
89. The Power of Stay Interviews
90. Developing G.R.I.T.
91. Adaptability
92. Diagnosis- *A Key Skill for Leadership*
93. The Burnout-Proof Salesperson: *The Master Guide to Preventing Stress & Burnout*- Strategies for Thriving in Sales
94. Learning from Failure: *Keys to Success*
95. Customer Success Management
96. Overcoming the Killers of Motivation
97. The C-Suite Code: *Mastering Skills for Executive Excellence'*

98. Dealing with Difficult Customers
99. Unlocking Your Potential: Mastering the Top 20 Life Skills for a Brighter Future
100. Nurturing Tomorrow's Leaders: *Essential Soft Skills Every Child Must Learn*
101. Lively & Fun Party Games for Seniors & Elders
102. Role Playing for Sales Champions: From Practice to Performance
103. Fun and Exciting Party Games for Kids
104. Case Studies for Sales
105. Role-Playing for Unbeatable Customer Service
106. Case Studies in Customer Service
107. Case Studies in Winning Negotiations
108. Case Studies in Management & Leadership
109. Case Studies in Human Resources & Talent Management
110. CEO Success Blueprint: The Essential Toolkit for CEOs and C-Level Executives
111. The Salesperson's Self-Coaching Guide: *Master Your Own Self-Coaching Plan for Success*
112. Overcoming Procrastination: *Your Ultimate Guide to Stop Delaying and Start Living Your Best Life*
113. When True Colors Are Exposed: *The Journey to Unmasking Humanity*
114. Life-Changing Habits for Teens: Teen Success Blueprint for a Bright Future
115. Workplace Stress-Free: *Proven Strategies to Thrive at Work and Beyond*
116. Objection Overruled: *The Ultimate Guide to Turning 'No' into 'Yes'*
117. Building Strong Teams: *A Comprehensive Guide to Team Building*
118. Ethical & Moral Leadership in Business: *Eliminating Unethical Practices & Building a Culture of Trust & Integrity*

From the Ministry side, Gerard graduated in the very first batch of Charis Bible College-India & had for over 9 years served as a Part-time Faculty at Charis Bible College-Chennai (Andrew Wommack Ministries-Colorado, USA). He also holds a Diploma in Worship (a subject closest to his heart) from the JSOW and is also a graduate of the Advanced Mentorship Program (AMP) and the Circle Of

Ministerial Engagement (C.O.M.E.) of Prophet Jerome Fernando and a Spiritual Son of the Esteemed Prophet. An accomplished author of several Secular & Christian Books, Gerard has been on the board of a few international organizations and boasts of being the SON of the MOST HIGH GOD: An ordinary guy following an extraordinary GOD!

...And some of his most recent Christian Books being:

1. A Bouquet of Praises for My KING
2. Christian Jokes for the Serious Religious' Folks!
3. Jesus Healed You!
4. Praise24Ever! (also in Tamil version)
5. The 5G Network of GOD
6. Building Faith over F.E.A.R- FACE EVERYTHING AND RISE with JESUS
7. Hebrew and Greek Praise and Worship Words
8. Godly Mothers' and Grandmothers' Bible Story time for Kids!
9. Miracles of Jesus in Pictures
10. Raise your Praise all 365 Days
11. Thanking GOD with an Attitude of Gratitude
12. Meditating on the Attributes of GOD
13. Puppet Scripts
14. Alcohol Ruins, JESUS Reforms, Renews & Restores!
15. Habakkuk 2:2 Christian Daily Journal, Planner & Organizer
16. ABC of GOD's Word for Handwriting Practice
17. Daily Bible Verse Handwriting Practice (Building Godly Character & Faith through Cursive Handwriting Practice!)
18. Guiding Light: Fun & Faith-Building Bible Activities for Children
19. Rejecting Grasshopper Talk: From Grasshopper to Giant-Killer-*Defeating Giants Daily!*
20. Teen Titans of Faith: *Building Courage, Determination & Christ-like-Esteem*
21. I AM Empowered: *Unleashing Divine Power with Positive Declarations*
22. Be A Solution Provider-*From Passion to Purpose: A Biblical Guide to Being the Answer to the World!*
23. Miracles of JESUS
24. Parables of Jesus for a Meaningful Life!
25. A Grateful Heart: Importance of Sharing Testimonies of GOD's Grace
26. Melodies of Worship to JESUS: 31 Songs of Praise & Worship From My Heart to HIS!
27. I AM SO BLESSED!
28. My Daily Cup of Energizer

29. 31 Leadership Lessons *from* Jesus- *The Supreme Leader*
30. Peace Amidst Storms: A Biblical Guide to Conquering S.T.R.E.S.S.
31. Rise Above: 20 Biblical Eagle Lessons for Life's Triumphs
32. Godly Goal Setting: *The FAITHFUL Blueprint for a Purpose-Driven Life*
33. The Profound Attributes of our Mighty GOD: Understanding the 10S's of the Almighty
34. Worship Now, Worship Forever: *A Journey from Earthly Praise to Eternal Glory*
35. Unceasing Praise & Worship: *365 Days to Worship the King*
36. The ROAR Within: *Living with Purpose and Authority through the Power of the Holy Spirit*
37. From Potential to Purpose: Unlocking and Multiplying Your Talents & Gifts for Kingdom Impact
38. Songs from the Heart: *Worshipping GOD in Your Own Tune & Melody*
39. Awakening Praise & Worship: Hebrew & Greek Words to Raise Your Praise
40. Sing a NEW Song to the LORD Everyday: *Daily Devotions of Praise & Worship to Lift Your Heart & Glorify HIS Name*
41. *The* A.R.O.M.A. of True Worship: *Creating Worship That Delights God*
42. Becoming A Kingdom Champion: *Embracing God's Call for a Life of Purpose & Victory*
43. The Busy Businessman's Daily Devotional: 366 Crisp Truths to Start Your Day Strong
44. The Teacher's Heart: *Daily Devotions for Educators*
45. Anchored! *A 31-Day Devotional for Students Facing Life's Challenges*
46. Suddenly! Unlocking Unorthodox Breakthroughs through Unusual Worship
47. Overcoming Adversity: *Lessons from the Bible for Modern Challenges*
48. LORD, Don't do it without me
49. Kingdom Leadership: *Biblical Principles for Modern Leaders*
50. Heartprints of God- *Growing God's Way:* Daily Devotions for Kids to Shine Bright
51. Send Judah First: Let your Praises Go up First to See the Mighty Move of GOD
52. DIVINE MOMENTS: *Recognizing, Embracing, Preparing, and Walking into Life-Changing Encounters with God*
53. Be a Builder in the Kingdom: *The C.E.M.E.N.T. Guide*

to Creating a Lasting Legacy

54. Unshakable: *Pillars of Godly Womanhood* (Pillars of Faith That Changed History)
55. Lead Like a Shepherd: *14 Essential Traits for Pastoral Excellence*
56. The Worship Leader's Arsenal: *Powerful Exhortations to Ignite Thanksgiving, Praise & Worship*
57. Women of UnShakable Faith: *31-Day Devotional for Strength, Purpose & Influence*
58. Called to Teach: *A Complete 10-Week Training Guide for Impactful VBS Teachers*
59. Strumming for the KING: Cowboy Songs of Faith & Fire
60. The Ultimate Youth Camp Playbook: *50 Bible-Centered Indoor Games to Engage, Equip, and Empower Teens*
61. Glad in HIS Presence: *David's Revelation of GOD's Love & Mercy*
62. The Spirit Behind the Sound: *52 Devotionals for Worship Teams*
63. THE COWBOY'S COMPASS: *Riding the Trail of Faith with Grit & Grace*
64. Worship as My Weapon: *Living Victoriously through the Power of Praise*
65. A Worshipper Always Wins: *Living a Life of Victorious Worship*
66. Worship That Leads to the Throne: *Practical Strategies for Worship Leaders to Inspire Their Team & Usher People into God's Presence*
67. Worship as Warfare: *Conquering through the Sound of Surrender*

Besides regularly contributing to business & trade journals, including international ones such as the 'Creative Training Techniques' and the 'Sales News' of the U.S.A, He is also a member of several prestigious bodies & trade associations, having participated in many Conferences & Workshops in India & Overseas.

Prior to his last assignment of leading & managing a large MNC as head, Gerard had a 3-year stint in the Middle East as a Consultant with a leading British

Consultancy Firm.

As the past 'Official Country Representative' for the International Business Award- 'THE STEVIES'-(the business world's own Oscar) for about 4 years- he ensured a few Indian companies that qualify for the same every year!

Gerard can be contacted at:
Email: training@Sales-Training.in,training@CollectionSkills.com
Websites:
www.Sales-Training.in
www.EtiquetteWorks.in
www.CollectionSkills.com
www.RetailSalesTraining.in
www.SalesTrainingIndia.com
www.ManualPreparation.com
www.TrainingWithPuppets.com
www.FirstContactAcademy.com
www.SalesAndMarketingRecruiter.com

www.ingramcontent.com/pod-product-compliance
Ingram Content Group UK Ltd.
Pitfield, Milton Keynes, MK11 3LW, UK
UKHW021340190726
13845UKWH00027B/647

9 788198 697455